Joachim Broecher
Creating Learning Spaces

Educational Research | Volume 1

Joachim Broecher lives in Berlin and is professor and director of the Department for the Education of Learners with Emotional, Social, and Behavioral Difficulties at the University of Flensburg, Germany. His research interests center around experiential education, urban studies, cultural mapping, and school culture development.

JOACHIM BROECHER
Creating Learning Spaces
Experiences from Educational Fields

[transcript]

Bibliographic information published by the Deutsche Nationalbibliothek
The Deutsche Nationalbibliothek lists this publication in the Deutsche Nationalbibliografie; detailed bibliographic data are available in the Internet at http://dnb.d-nb.de

© 2019 transcript Verlag, Bielefeld

All rights reserved. No part of this book may be reprinted or reproduced or utilized in any form or by any electronic, mechanical, or other means, now known or hereafter invented, including photocopying and recording, or in any information storage or retrieval system, without permission in writing from the publisher.

Cover layout: Maria Arndt, Bielefeld
Translated by Dirk Siepmann, Osnabrück
Typeset by Joachim Broecher
Printed by Majuskel Medienproduktion GmbH, Wetzlar
Print-ISBN 978-3-8376-4887-4
PDF-ISBN 978-3-8394-4887-8
https://doi.org/10.14361/9783839448878

Content

Preface | 7

1 Teaching on the Frontline | 11

2 Maladjusted Youth as Sand in the Gears? | 41

3 Accessing Art with Movable Layout | 55

4 Challenging Disabling School Policies | 73

5 When Children Plan a Trip on Their Own | 91

6 Experiential Learning Across the Fields | 115

References | 151

Preface

This volume assembles experiences from the areas of early childhood education, gifted education, special education, inclusive education, and adult education. These happen in a variety of locales, such as summer camps, school settings, family settings and projects.

The first chapter focuses on the work situation of a special education teacher, who upon arriving in an urban school for students with behavioral difficulties, began keeping a journal which spanned his first three months at work. Using qualitative content analysis, his field notes were organized by subject areas and examined with reference to the patterns that emerged. The results provide insights into a challenging educational reality. I would like to thank Nicola Kluge, Woodlands, Texas, for her support during the analysis of the data which is documented in this chapter. Nicola and I presented and discussed the results of our analysis at the 2013 annual conference of the »Council for Children with Behavioral Disorders (CCBD)«, in Chicago.

The second chapter recounts the journey of a special education teacher traveling by train with his class to the North Sea island of Sylt, in Germany, where the group intends to spend a week in a school camp. During the journey, various incidents and upsets take place that escalate to the uncoupling of a train car. This real episode was used productively for several years in special education university courses, such as inclusive education, for the purpose of storytelling as a pedagogical tool in higher education.

Chapter three deals with the »Movable Layout Technique (MLT)«, an instructional adaptation here used to teach art in challenging classrooms. With MLT students with social, emotional, and behavioral difficulties unexpectedly find themselves in a complex process of designing, experimenting and composing. They are easily and successfully guided into the artistic terrain and encouraged to independently lay out pictures and creative compositions in a motivational and pleasurable way. With MLT students advance gradually to complex picture composition and spatial organization, opening up pathways to freer forms of artistic work.

The fourth chapter explores the »Training Room Program (TRP)«, a time-out model that is based on the American »Responsible Thinking Process (RTP)«. Since 2003 this model has become established in German schools in response to students' increasingly challenging learning and social behavior. School administrators and academics alike recommend the implementation of the TRP as part of their efforts to conform to one of the goals put forth in the UN convention of ensuring the success of inclusive schooling for students with behavioral difficulties. But in executing this model, formal inclusion and temporary exclusion within the school become interconnected. The results yielded by this program evaluation indicate that the program impedes the development of a participative and empowering learning culture, even though it is precisely this factor which is indispensable for the successful inclusion of learners with emotional and social needs.

The focus of chapter five is education within families. The father in this case study gave each of his two sons a voucher for a one-week trip that the boys would each plan, then take separately with the father during the upcoming summer vacation. The father collected his initial thought processes and the plans in journal form. Together they reread journals from earlier trips and reflected on what happened in their course. Here the two journeys planned by the children are examined and discussed using qualitative textual analysis with the findings are linked to current theoretical knowledge.

Anyone who has accumulated wide ranging experiences in teaching faces a creative choice in putting that legacy to paper. I myself, in this case, chose to use a series of photos with text to illustrate formative and inspirational moments from my several decades as a dedicated teacher, and father. My account (chapter 6) begins with university studies in special and gifted education, followed by years of teaching school while living a fulfilling family life with my wife and two boys. These experiences culminate with my pedagogical research activities in the field of higher education coupled, in part, with retrospective reflections during these later years. The chapter closes with selected material from an intergenerational learning project that served to put me in touch once more with my own roots.

Most notably, I would like to thank Dirk Siepmann and his team from University of Osnabrück, Germany, for translating this very particular compilation of texts which I selected for this volume.

This book is dedicated to my wife Karin Anna Jung-Bröcher, in gratitude for her loving companionship and support through all these years. She herself is a long-time special education teacher in an inclusive elementary school and, at the same time, always a devoted mother to our sons. Finally I would like to express my special thanks to my sons, in gratitude for their faithful companionship and all the shared learning that we could experience together. Karin and the boys also made substantial contributions to the chapters 5 and 6. I thank them all. J.B.

1 Teaching on the Frontline

The positive effects of journal writing in the context of teacher preparation and teacher training are well documented (e.g., Dieker and Monda-Amaya, 1995; Gilar et al., 2007; Jarvis, 1992). Here a special education teacher started a journal upon commencing work at a large German city's specialized school to help him cope with the transition. At that time, he had more than 12 years professional experience. The journal covers the first 95 work days at the new school. During the first 33 work days, the teacher made daily entries without interruption followed by a lengthy hiatus lasting 36 work days. Finally, he started making entries again sporadically summarizing events on work days 70-95 (Fig. 1.1). There the journal ends. These »field notes« (Patton 2002, p. 302) offer insights into a challenging pedagogical world. The teacher made his journal available for a scholarly evaluation.

The several perspectives from which we can view these journal contents can be viewed yield the following questions for research: What student behavior is displayed here? What didactic and pedagogical strategies does the teacher employ and how can these be made still more effective? How does the journal-keeping teacher reflect on his educational work and how could one-on-one coaching provide him with effective support? What do we learn about the school culture as a whole and how it could be improved to better support the teacher's efforts in the classroom?

With regard to the first research question, an extensive literature shows that students with emotional and social needs often do not work on the tasks assigned by the teacher, that their behavior interrupts the lesson if it does not shut it down completely, and that they often provoke conflicts during class with other students and teachers (e.g., Kauffman and Landrum, 2011; Stichter et al., 2008), depending on how well developed the individual students' coping strategies (e.g., McSherry 2013) are. The situation is exacerbated by the concurrent existence of learning problems (e.g., Algozzine et al., 2011; Nicholson 2014).

Seen as helpful and effective, and hence as the backdrop for the second research question, is a caring teacher-student relationship (e.g., Cefai 2013; Cooper 2011; Garza 2009; Kniveton 2004), responding with sensitivity to the developmental needs of the students (e.g., Boorn et al., 2010; Boxall 2010; Colley 2009; Doyle 2003), tuning into the students' life experiences and learning preferences (e.g., O'Connor et al., 2011), and a teaching approach that also makes use of humor (e.g., Rogers 2013) in case of doubt. The teaching of social skills and emotional literacy (e.g., Kavale et al., 2004; Rae 2012) and teaching self-regulation (e.g., Mowat 2010) are additional action approaches holding the promise for success. In didactic terms, the following is held to be effective: employing variable and differentiated learning methods (e.g., Kern et al., 2001; Popp et al., 2011), reducing the level of task difficulty and the task duration in order to decrease escape-motivated problem behavior (e.g., Lee et al., 1999; Moore et al., 2005), offering opportunities to respond (e.g., Haydon et al., 2012), offering choices (e.g., Shogren et al., 2004) and, finally, giving behavior-specific praise (e.g., Marchant and Anderson, 2012). All pedagogical and didactic strategies must be carefully tailored to the specific context of a learning group (Conroy et al., 2014).

With regard to the third research question, we can fall back on a literature that addresses reflection on one's own educational practices (e.g., Schön 1983), teacher self-awareness and teacher resilience (e.g., Howard and Johnson, 2004; Richardson and Shupe, 2003; Skovolt and Trotter-Mathison, 2011) as well as coaching and performance feedback (e.g., Lane et al., 2014). The goal always remains the same: Reinforce the individual teacher's professionalism and optimize the application of available know-how, here in the field of teaching students with emotional and social difficulties (Anderson-DeMello and Hendrickson, 2014). A solution-focused approach (e.g., Rae 2012) adds a great deal of value to this. Coach-the-teacher then is geared to the question of what works well. Fourth, looking at the school's overall culture, a key factor is involving the parents in all school-related issues (e.g., Ogden 2013; Sheldon and Epstein, 2002). Segregating their schooling in self-contained classrooms may impair the students' opportunities for social communication and participation (Panacek and Dunlap, 2003). The active involvement of the surrounding school community (e.g., Klein 2000) in school life therefore seems all the more significant. Support for the individual teacher by his colleagues and a dedicated principal (e.g., Blase and Blase, 2004; Blase and Kirby, 2009; Gamman 2003; Gardiner and Enomoto, 2006), either through joint supervision or reflection and the development of school-wide strategies, are indispensable. Further, well-developed interprofessional work (e.g., Eber and Keenan, 2004; Hamill and Boyd, 2001; O'Connor 2013) and an after-school program that offers stability and direction and, at the same time, relevant learning opportunities specifically to students in this field (e.g., Woodland 2008) are important pillars of a school culture that effectively supports the work of teachers in the classrooms.

To answer the research questions defined at the start, the field notes were subjected to a document analysis. For objectivity's sake, a second researcher worked in parallel, carrying out every step independently herself. The two researchers compared results. The content analysis filtered »themes« and »patterns« (Patton 2002) from the journal text. To this end, the text of 28,700 words was first divided into the smallest possible meaningful units. The next step dealt with labeling themes and assigning the material to these overarching thematic categories (Fig. 1.2). This was followed by finding patterns within the thematic areas.

The »case study« (Bassey 1999; Eisenhardt and Graebner, 2007; Flyvberg, 2011; Patton, 2002, pp. 447-452; Stake, 2005; Yin, 2009) also serves as a point of reference here, for threaded through this teacher's journal in effect are eight interwoven student cases. What follows is an overview of the themes and patterns that were found. These are illustrated by way of sample excerpts from the teacher's journal.

Description of the working conditions prevailing at this school takes up 4% of the entire journal: »... brief handover talk with the departing classroom teacher... I am taking over five of his students, with three new students from outside to be added, all of them between 14 and 16 years old... I will teach for 27.5 hours. Weekly... three schoolyard supervisions of thirty minutes each... I work alone in my classroom throughout. Every week, I can send a small group of students to departmental colleagues in the media classroom and shop classroom. There is a... billiards room... gym... foosball room and... school kitchen (day 2).«

Description of student behavior makes up nearly one-third (31%) of the journal text. Sorting all related patterns, 400 (62%) belong to the disruptive category and 242 (37%) to the constructive group. Nine cases (1%) are mixed, e.g.: »Leon is busily filing away... at a piece of wood that he found outside in front of the school. He is making one end pointed like a spear. As file, he is using a screw that he had fished out of my junk drawer. Working with such simple means, he says, reminds him of the survival strategies of the Huns... he wraps one end of the piece of wood with bast fiber, and now he has an archaic-looking hand weapon (day 13).«

Let us take a look at problematic patterns of student behavior (Fig. 1.3). With 22% not abiding by school rules is the most-frequently encountered pattern. Individually, this means: being late, leaving early, leaving school premises during recess. The frequency trend line for these patterns over the 95 days slopes slightly upward: »Patrick takes off without permission after recess (day 11)... Max drops out of sight, Patrick also disappears (day 16)... Acatey walks out of the individual class set up for him after a few minutes (day 28)... Dominic, Max, Tim and Leon for days already have been leaving the school grounds during yard recess and roam around the shopping street (day 29)... Jonas presumably has been truant for days already. He has a cough, he says on the phone. During the past year, Jonas has missed more than 70% of school days (day 33)... Patrick's cell phone rings, and he is gone (day 80).«

The behavioral pattern acting aggressively toward other students can exhibit itself verbally and/or physically. It is also highly represented with 21%: »Acatey holds Fabian's book bag out the window and drops it... Acatey hurls the ball... straight into Tim's face... to the bike shed with Fabian, to unlock his bike for him. Acatey squeezes in between us and rides off on Fabian's bike, disappearing into the city (day 7)... Acatey strikes at Patrick's head as he stands in front of the window. The latter's head hits the window frame. Furious, Patrick attacks Acatey (day 14)... Acatey... tries constantly to provoke Leon, by hitting or kicking, or waving his hands or fist in front of his face, pretending to kick his head... gets very close to Leon's face, gathers spittle in his mouth and makes as if he is going to spit it at him... hurls curses at Leon: ›Fuck your mother! Your mother is a whore. You freak! Your mother crapped you!‹ (day 15)... The computer network cables are ripped out. Loud yelling and carrying on« (day 30).

Actively rejecting curricular learning registers at 18%. The trend line shows a marked downward slope (Fig. 1.4). »Nobody wants to work on the assignment sheets passed out (day 3)... The first one refuses. The next one reads a couple of sentences and stops... then Max throws his notebook, nearly hitting my head: ›Here, you can have it back!‹ Three, four more notebooks land on my desk (day 4)... the boys work maybe three to eight minutes. Max complains his sheet is too easy. ›I won't do it, don't want to, give me something more difficult; naw, now that is too difficult for me, I'm not doing it‹, throws the sheet on the floor... It's all over with the others, too (day 6)... Leon protests... when I pass out the homework (day 14)... The boys refuse to take out their work folders and books... Fabian gives subtraction on paper a try, but gives up already after five minutes... He will not accept any help (day 15)... ›I want to get on the PC and play; I'm bored‹... that Fabian has not filled out a single part of the English Level 1 work book from the previous school year... ›So what, it's all boring, can I go now?‹ (day 18).«

Acting aggressively toward the teacher as another disruptive pattern, expressed verbally and/or physically, was determined in 16% of cases: »Patrick swears at me: ›Hey, you jackass! You mongoloid!‹ (day 11). Max... turns up his cell phone, it is a screeching, shrill piece of music... He says: ›What's your problem? I'll punch you in the face in a second!‹ (day 15)... Acatey... ›What did you talk about with my mother? I'll sock you!‹... (day 19)... While I sit next to Fabian to show him written division, Acatey waves the broomstick behind my head (day 19)... Patrick attacks me, what's with ›all this queer jabbering‹, and what do I care how they are doing. Tim... he would love to beat me up good for all the ›crap‹ we are doing during class here... moves his hands and arms karate-style. ›You're just fucking with me‹... Acatey demands to be returned to regular class. ›Freak! German potato! Rat fag!‹ he hisses at me (day 28)... Leon says to me: ›Freak, you can suck my big one!... I have nothing to say to you, you joker!‹ (day 32)... Leon threatens to beat me up if I dare to give him a new weekly lesson plan (day 33).«

Destroying learning materials and objects makes up 14% of the disruptive student behavior recorded by the teacher. The trend line clearly points down (Fig. 1.5): »Numerous objects fly out the window ... the classroom is on the 4th floor and the ceiling is very high... dishes, books, paper, notebooks... food... the sink is plugged up with glue and overflows (day 3)... Acatey rips a door from the cabinet that has a locker for each student (day 7)... Fabian with a piece of wood knocks stucco off places where the walls are already damaged. ›So what, what's your problem? They're going to renovate in here anyway‹, he says (day 10).«

Disruptive behavior in the wider community was a factor 5% of the time: »While I pay, Acatey and Fabian steal cones behind the ice cream seller's back... Fabian jostles an oncoming man... Fabian, with a smile, asks a woman if he can pet her dog... then pulls the yowling beast by its tail... the boys want to go to the cathedral... they go to a side altar and blow out dozens of candles... Acatey has seized on an offering box and is shaking it... to get at the coins inside... heads over to the candles again and spits the flame out on two of them... by the Rhine river promenade, they pull each other into a fountain (day 3)... Acatey tears open the door to a midday care center. Children are playing with beads and blocks... Acatey sweeps everything off the table (day 14)... Acatey... puts down fifty Euro and says: ›From a cell phone, with camera, ripped off... in... sold...‹ (day 15)... Leon, Max and Tim... threatened the owner of a health food store... when she asks them if she can help with anything else, they say no, but still do not leave the store... when the owner asked the boys to leave the store... Leon walked up to her and said: ›You're about to get a punch in the mouth‹ (day 31)... Fabian... gives a parked car a kick. A colleague reports... that he had slammed a shopping cart against a parked car; then he jumped on the hood of another car (day 80).«

In 2% of the cases, the students ignored the teacher's specific instructions: »While driving the pedal cars, Acatey once more disregards the rules, crosses the threshold, purposely crashes into the others, drives through the door out on the street (day 11)... Max, during recess, climbs on top of the toilet house, and runs around on it (day 12)... Acatey shows up too early, he is trying to sabotage the new class schedule. He is also not ready to leave again (day 15)... as soon as the computers are up... games are booted up: Counterstrike and Döner-Mafia (day 30).«

In a further 2% of cases, the teacher had to deal with really dangerous behaviors by his students: »Twice, Max tosses a chair (with iron frame) against the wall (day 3)... Acatey runs over a first grader with the heavy pedal car while the teacher was crossing the schoolyard to the gym with her charges (day 6)... Leon is at the window sill... suddenly, a giant flame almost sets the curtain ablaze. He had wrapped a ping pong ball in aluminum foil and... lit it with a lighter (day 18)... Leon opens firecrackers, pretends he wants to examine the powder and finally pours it into a tennis ball. He fills the remaining empty space with thin paper and mounts a fuse on it (day 29)... Leon carries hair spray in his pocket... A... jet of fire shoots through the room (day 31).«

We now turn to the 242 constructive patterns in student behavior (37%). Figure 1.6 shows how the patterns were differentiated by categories. With 31% willingness to engage in curricular learning is the constructive behavior most often encountered among the students. The trend line drops slightly: »Tim and Dominic participate in a half hour of English instruction (day 7)... It goes well for about twenty minutes. Then the boys want to get on the computer (day 13)... They actually begin to do math (day 14)... Acatey works along well today during the individual mentoring. After forty minutes, the air has gone out of him (day 30). They mostly take the weekly lesson plans home now and work on them more or less thoroughly... between 5% and 70%, on the daily plans 5% and 40% (day 72).«

Fifteen percent of cases fit the pattern communicating positively with other students: »Some of the boys have not breakfasted and want to go buy buns and cold cuts. When they return, they set the round table in back of the classroom (day 13)... Leon has brought buns to be heated... Because no one had yet done the dishes and cutlery, an improvised breakfast is served on a stolen tabloid newspaper on my desk, because the boys opine that it was the cleanest place. Margarine and chocolate spread... are ladled on with the finger, ›just like in a Hun encampment‹, Leon says (day 18).«

Following school rules (attendance) becomes visible in 14% of cases, the teacher took the trouble to note that certain students were in class. This shows a slightly decreasing tendency. Twelve percent of positive patterns relate to quiet, constructive behavior by the students during low-threshold, self-determined activities such as computer games, listening to music or playing foosball.

Reflecting on own behaviors and life backgrounds factored in 12% of the time. The trend line climbs slightly: »Can you picture it, how he beat me, my father? For years... He drank his fill and then he always started in... I swear, nothing was going on between that man and my mother... There my father stood in the doorway, legs apart... my mother told him that she was so tired... ›Yes, from screwing!‹ says my father... He goes for her. ›Don't you hit her‹, I said, ›I'll kill you!‹ But, he keeps after her and hits her in the face, several times. She is bleeding... she tears open a drawer... takes out a long knife and says to him: ›All right, come on!‹ I run outside, take my cell phone and call the police... my father is lying on the floor, gurgling... I was totally out of it, my mother in the corner, totally done in, shaking, crying« (Leon on day 25)... »Tim asks me, if I knew what ›psychological stress‹ is. A friend of his supposedly has it, so his doctor had told him. And that's why he still bed wets at night, at the age of thirteen. He himself had the same problem for quite a while. Did I have any advice for his friend by chance? (day 90).«

Building a positive relationship with the teacher was encountered in 9% of cases, with a slightly falling trend line: »Patrick shows me a picture of his attack dog... Then he offers me peanuts (day 3)... Leon tells me about his life as part of a Hun horde... that his identity was largely that of a Hun... his shock of dark hair, standing up on his head, long in back and shaved at the temples, emphasizes it (day 12)... I am invited to join an improvised breakfast. Tim insists that I also take a bun (day 13)... leafed through the Guinness Book of Records with Patrick and Leon. Leon lies to left of me on the side table and Patrick stands immediately to my right... we... comment on the pictures... Patrick smiles... friendly... there follow tentative touches to my hand, my arm or my shoulder (day 13)... Leon rides a skateboard... constantly, he calls out to me. ›Look at me... Look at me...‹ (day 15)... Leon meanwhile crisps his bread, and then mine also. He insists on doing this for me (day 16)... Leon rides skateboard again and constantly wants my attention, also physical touching, with me pushing him. This moves Patrick to pat me on the back and shoulder several times; this, from the same Patrick who usually avoids all physical contact (day 17)... Leon asks me if I have any chap stick, his lips were so dry (day 26).«

Asking the teacher for help, assistance or shelter was found in 5% of cases: »The new students seek sanctuary and protection with me, even if in disguised fashion (day 3)... Leon says he is afraid of getting into fights and so wants to stay close to me all the time (day 10)... Leon is still afraid and wants to sit in the office when I am not on the yard (day 11)... Leon... stays... in my vicinity in the school yard (day 13).«

Exhibiting successful emotional self-control shows up in 2% of cases: »Acatey can't get on the PCs, because of passwords set by the other students. He succeeds in maintaining control of himself (day 30).«

Positives and negatives lie close together and interlock: »Acatey invariably buys breakfast only for himself; now and then he shares some candy, but tosses it over so... contemptuously... that the others do not accept the stuff. Max, Dominic, Tim and Leon, in contrast, develop first solidarity arrangements among themselves; different students alternate, even if irregularly, in bringing something to eat and sharing with the others... When Acatey sits at his desk and eats whatever he has brought... he does so with loud smacking noises, something the others have a hard time putting up with (day 20).«

The positive can quickly tip into the destructive: »Leon devises a plan for a ›cozy kitchen corner‹, with food and drinks in the refrigerator to be bought out of a common kitty. ›When the others are ready, I mean, when they don't destroy or throw stuff around, then...‹ Acatey... provokes Leon... This time, Leon loses his cool and he shouts furiously at Acatey: ›For once, just shut your mouth, you damn foreigner! They must have crapped you out, huh? One of these days we'll wipe all our damn foreigners out!‹ and raises a chair and threatens to throw it at Acatey (day 16)... (in the billiard room)... We have been playing for three or four minutes, when Acatey's constructive mood suddenly turns. He hits the white ball so hard that it bounds over the table edge and shoots in the direction of my face. All the while, he grins at me out of his dark, glittering eyes. Acatey changes his stance, so get a better shot at me. Then he waves the queue in front of my face as if about to hit me with it (day 23).«

Ambiguous situations can be productive but require coolness and vision: »Leon has brought in a condom, fills it with water, knots it and plays with it... He reads attentively what I write on a poster, while he sits cross-legged to my right on the table... Leon raises the water filled condom to his mouth and sucks on it... Leon suddenly stands behind me and touches me on the throat, ears, neck with this phallic symbol... He does all this in a joking... way. Then he splats the water filled condom against my thigh so that it bursts. Leon contorts with laughter, but at the same time he seems embarrassed, and he apologizes (day 24)... Then Leon takes two... tables... shoves them up against the sides of my desk, lies across them... pensively sucks and draws on the water filled condom... Then he says: ›Oh, crap, my life is really messed up. I'm in an institution and then here, in this school, what kind of life am I going to have?... I've thought about jumping off a bridge‹ (day 25).«

Behavioral progress takes time: »Fabian is eating candy again and drops the wrappers on the floor. He picks them up unwillingly at the end of the class, but instead of throwing them into the waste basket purposely misses it. Finally, he does pick up some of the papers again. He leaves the rest on the floor (day 16)... Max is still spitting pumpkin seed shells on the floor, but more and more frequently directly into the waste basket (day 85).«

In a few instances, a student helps the teacher clarify his pedagogic concern, however, in a language suitable for precipitating the next conflict among the students: »Patrick: ›You idiot, you bastard, you fly shit, didn't you get it? He means that you are responsible for what you learn here! Get it?!‹ (day 25).«

The documented teacher's behavior corresponds to almost the same extent (31%) with the comprehensively described student behavior. This we broke down into several patterns (Fig. 1.7). In 30% of the cases, the teacher is busy containing transgressive or destructive behavior: »The boys... are kicking the ball around the classroom. I... lock the ball up again (day 4)... then I grab the chair and pull it down... to the floor again (day 10)... I announce that I will send Max home immediately if he tears my seating arrangement up again... ›It is not acceptable to speak with me in that tone of voice...‹ I ask him to turn off the music (day 15)... This time, I insist that Fabian picks up all the candy wrappers (day 16)... I approach Acatey determinedly and tell him that I do not like his game (day 23)... I plant myself in front of Acatey... will he ›manage today to abide by three rules: no insults, no physical contact with another, no damaging anything?‹ (day 25)... Acatey demands to be returned to the regular classes. I tell him the conditions (day 28)... one day suspension from school for Leon, for reason of the hairspray and flame jet (day 32).«

Fostering curricular learning and implementing learning assessment is represented with 24%: »I choose a text about friendships in a clique and ask the students to read (day 4)... pass out math sheets at differing levels of difficulty (day 6)... test his knowledge and skills in math and English... grade Leon's first homework assignment... exchange a more difficult text book for Leon's English book (day 10)... propose to delve into the Hun subject as part of school work (day 12)... try to be in better tune with the boys' actual math skills, test Tim's learning level (day 15)... Leon is interested in geometry, so we skip around in the book a bit (day 18)... I come up with the idea of taking what Leon said... developing it... into questions for research (day 24)... I engage the youths... in discussions about computer games... what they think about the effect of games on perceptions and behavior of the players (day 30)... discussion about Preußler's book ›Krabat‹... how far they have read in it, what they find interesting in it, where they are having difficulty understanding, I paint a poster... with the names of the fictional characters (day 33)... Next... step by step got the students... used to a weekly lesson plan, with regard to homework... The challenges... are widely varied, so that there is... something for every ability level in it... Later, I introduced... additionally daily lesson plans, in order to give the morning a firm but flexible structure (day 72)... I spoke about performance evaluations... that there would be objective content requirements for the various subjects, and I provide an overview for math, biology and English... to give them a chance to recognize their own performance level (day 75).«

The pattern exploring and reflecting the students' world was represented at 10%: »I start by talking about getting acquainted. I thought about a kind of chart for self-presentation... categories like interests, neighborhood, and age (day 3)... a discussion about experiences during summer vacation (day 5)... I speak extensively with Leon about the Hun horde... to which he belongs (day 12)... I ask the new arrivals how they are doing, how they spent the afternoon the day before and the evening (day 16).«

Teaching and acknowledging positive behavior occurred in 9% of cases: »I thank Dominic for his cooperation (day 5)... Acatey worked for ten minutes on problems he picked out himself from the math book. I praise him for this (day 11)... I repeatedly speak with Leon about not letting himself be lured into a brawl with Acatey and give him praise for already having restrained himself for so long... Later, corrected Fabian's essay. I praised him for doing the work (day 16)... To Max: ›Did you not see a chance to come to Gerrit's aid or to at least exert a calming influence on the situation?‹ (day 19)... To Leon: ›Your great strength is that you can think so well about yourself and about everything that goes on inside you, that you are aware of these things‹ (day 25)... I boil water... and rinse the breakfast dishes... Does he ever help out in the kitchen at home, I ask Acatey... ›Wouldn't you like to sweep up? That way, you also have something to do. Besides, then I'll be finished faster and we can read something together‹ (day 27). I brought a Jiu-Jitsu trainer to class with me. The trainer and I acted as if we were provoking each other, then used different defensive techniques, he from Jiu-Jitsu, me from Tai Chi... we discussed aspects such as... inner strength, controlling one's own aggression, self-discipline, protecting one's own private space, and simply walking away at times (day 90).«

Developing learning motivation and future perspectives was found as a pattern in 8% of the teacher interventions: »I take up the wish of resuming schooling in a mainstream school and encourage the boys not to let up from applying themselves to their work (day 7)... Asked Max today about his perspective on job prospects, wants to ›turn tricks as whore at the train station‹ (day 14)... talk with Leon about his career goals... I suggest looking into which job specifications touch on his interests... e.g., electric equipment installer, electronic technician for drive technology, what the job descriptions are for these professions, what the training prerequisites and requirements are (day 25).«

Creating and maintaining classroom order and a healthy learning environment was found in 7% of cases: »In the cabinets, I lock up anything I can grab, so that everything does not go sailing out the windows... there is still sweeping up, with a borrowed broom (day 3)... I set up a schedule who can go when to the shop room and the media room (day 9)... I inform them about the new regime with the second time-shifted lesson plan (day 11)... I take Tim and Dominic with me... to buy... broom, hand broom, dustpan, rinsing bowl, dishwashing liquid, and a new binder for each student (day 17)... I obtained green plants and put them on the window sills. In the back of the classroom, I put up natural science maps of fauna and flora and a teaching poster with all ship types (day 24).«

Building positive teacher-student relationships was a 7% factor: »I invite the boys out for ice cream (day 3)... I continually get... students from the two classrooms adjoining mine on either side. I take the opportunity to start a conversation with these boys as well (day 4)... I absolutely must sit down for this... I bring a teapot and buttered bread with me and sit down with the four of them. Tim insists that I also take a bun (day 13)... I ask Max and the others how they are getting along (day 15)... Leon crisps his bread in the meantime, later mine as well. He insists on doing this for me (day 16)... I bring more green plants to the classroom, sweep, wipe bookshelves, window sills, and tables with a moist cloth, rinse drinking cups, boil water, make lemon tea for the boys... create a familial ambiance (day 85).«

Clarifying group conflicts was found in 5% of cases: »Back in the classroom, I try to unwind the conflict between Acatey and Patrick (day 14)... after a short rest period the opponents spend in separate classrooms, we succeed in clearing up what happened and the interior process (day 17)... We end the talk with the agreement that they would avoid each other and should their paths cross, not to start arguing (day 19)... I also prepare two posters, one in orange, the other in yellow. This time with the headings ›external complaints‹ and ›inner complaints‹ (day 24)... As I am trying to pull apart two scufflers tied up in each other, Leon tries to stop me from doing so. First, I have to shake him off before I can intervene in the heated struggle of the two boys now fighting on the ground, already ringed by... spectators (day 30).«

The teacher's thoughts, emotions and reflections as another theme makes up 13% of the teacher's journal entries. We differentiated among the following patterns (Fig. 1.8): Seeing through and beyond the student behavior occurred in almost 30% of cases: »Why the wanton throwing of stuff out the window?... Establishing a hierarchy among one themselves?... To let go... of the teacher left?... Find out how I react to these things? (day 3)... Neither of the two budges. Perhaps it would mean a loss of face... Acatey hangs on... to Patrick, although... physically the weaker. It is as if he was inviting... the punches and kicks... every few days he has blue splotches on his face (day 14)... The first, deeper-going relations take root among the students over the communal breakfast... that Acatey will not be asked to join in anymore, because he has blown it with this group... It is also possible that he does not find any kind of model for this kind of social interaction within himself (day 20). Leon has now emerged for good from my protective shadow and has changed sides. He starts to continually attack and insult me in front of the other students... he wants to arrive once and for all in the group of classmates and be accepted in it (day 30).«

Reflecting and clarifying self-perceptions and own emotions was encountered in 19% of cases: »I'm becoming uneasy (day 3)... the boys are as big as me and even with Tai Chi and fitness training, I do not want risk any physical altercations (day 5)... near-chaos (day 10)... Acatey takes my backpack, and, stupidly, in that class that day my valuables happen to be in it... the students have several times removed my bundle of keys from the desk. A... game, that... is nerve wracking (day 14)... The situation is improving... Hopefully, Acatey will not come in early again... recess is relatively peaceful (day 17)... For a few minutes at least, no outside violations (day 18)... Still, it makes me nervous. Somehow, I blame it on the system for not remedying the chronic staff shortage and seemingly being unconcerned with how I'm going to survive each round under these conditions (day 19).«

Pedagogical and didactical planning is present 12% of the time: »Locking the door and sending the boys who do not belong to my own class away... would... signal rejection (day 4)... In this group setting, which themes... deserve to be stressed?... I visualize what I observe... I describe moderation charts... and hang the charts in the... topic tracker: ›to really make an effort and learn something, set goals for yourself, leave all things intact, make use of the teacher's learning offerings, everyone here is special, everyone here is likable, respect others... follow the rules, rule violations have consequences, respect the other's boundaries, be on time for class, formulate learning interests, feel secure, feel good, be polite, do your homework, help each other, become a group, be at ease sitting around in a group, be in the present moment here. See how the boys react to this?‹ (day 20).«

Evaluating the effectiveness of own actions occurred in 11% of cases: »I start with a success, a bit of order... to be maintained (day 15)... It is hard to pull the two bodies locked into each other apart. Finally, I succeed (day 17)... I hold out the prospect that every properly completed assignment sheet will get credit for grading purposes. This seems to motivate some (day 18)... Acatey... furious ›I'll slug you!‹... ›No, you won't‹, I tell him loud and clear. At the same time, I assume a defensive posture derived from Tai Chi. The message hits home (day 19).«

Planning behavior-related interventions factors in 9% of the time: »... slam the door shut, stick the key in the lock and lock it from the inside. This all has to happen very quickly... It is important that no one feels locked up. Locking a rampaging student out is a matter of self-protection and protection of the other students (day 19)... perhaps, make a start by preparing a meal together with Acatey and then eat it together with him and... then invite another student and another... (day 20).«

Analyzing teaching and learning processes was found in 8% of cases: »Holding a regular class is still out of the question (day 11)... that Max simply just copies all results... for the moment... is secondary, I think... homework... For all the others, this is still out of the question. They would do nothing with it (day 14)... I regard... the external chaos caused by the students as a reflection of their inner psychic situation. It makes no sense at this point to ask them to keep themselves in check and to help with sweeping, etc. (day 19)... Acatey... is excluded from the circle of the other classmates, because he simply cannot manage to control his destructive impulses (day 20)... The learning and work behavior had to be built up among the students... from scratch (day 72).«

Dealing with pedagogical dilemmata occurred in 6% of cases: »... what effects would my working with the police have on the quality of my pedagogical relationship with... the... boys, when almost every one of them engages in small-time criminal actions? (day 15)... Max goes to the bathroom... for a smoke? I am glad he is so peaceable today (day 19).

Still urgently have to study... the files... On the other hand, I shy away from it, because after reading these... statements, reports and expert opinions, all the notations are crimes and court dates... I no longer regard the boys without prejudice (day 19). Prohibit... Counterstrike... or thematize it? (day 30)... Döner-Mafia... Was that game... the template for the boys' performance in the health food store? (day 31)... The past year, Jonas has missed more than 70% of school days. Would a mandatory court appearance even do any good? (day 33)... Patrick is becoming softer, more trusting toward me... his father comes on like a Mafia boss. Meanwhile, I've gotten credit from both of them because I relegate everything that is not immediately related to... school to being a family matter, which I steer clear of completely. It is harder for the social worker... Patrick says the man talks too much (day 80).«

Reflecting on teacher-student relationships cropped up in 5% of cases: »... small... talk with the boys from the class next door... this way they feel someone is paying attention to them (day 5)... I sit down in the reading corner with Acatey... some days he appears to be downright fragile and to need support (day 13)... Max... sits cross legged on my desk... As if he wanted to say: ›Look at me! Here I am!‹... He never dared come that close to me before. He acts as if he wants to ram his fist in my face (day 24).«

Collaborating with fellow teachers and the principal as thematic area comprises 9% of the journal text: »The boys are now asking me for a soft ball... to play soccer in the hallway... I check this out with a colleague and learn that it is customary, for relaxation... to let the students... play soccer in the hallway... the colleague from the media room asks... if we had book requisitions (day 4)... here, all colleagues advise against bringing valuable items to the classrooms (day 10). Once again, a colleague had her new cell phone stolen from the teacher's lounge... The students are to arrive in shifts after the weekend in order to rectify the situation. The tip came from colleagues, all supported it in the teacher conference, including the principal (day 10)... Case consultation. I ask the colleagues to tell me about the four *old* students in my class (day

12)... The principal's view is that it is not about exerting power, but instead about acting consistently, for example: If you are going to break off the cabinet door, you will have to pay for it. Then we will ask your father to come and discuss what else remains to be done. So, think about what you are doing. This way, you put the responsibility on the youngster. The principal counsels against breaking ground in too many places and to concentrate foremost on the subject of reparations... The next subject to be thematized could be leaving class without permission. If I am not in a position to devote myself intensively to this construction site then I would do better... to hold off for now (day 13). The teacher next door needs a clean cloth... I send one over to her (day 15)... Visits during class time must be reduced. As a tentative solution we settle on leaving the doors open for a quarter of an hour before class starts to leave the students space for contacts... with each other (day 18)... Together with the principal and teaching staff, I decided that Acatey would no longer take part in regular classroom instruction. He will get three hours individual support from me... other than that, we will let everything that to date has functioned continue to run for him..., an hour of soccer with another class and the moped course (day 27).«

A total of 8% of the journal text falls under the theme collaborating with parents or guardians: »Leon's mother tells me this evening on the phone that I've gotten too close emotionally to her son, which he is having to compensate for by stepping up his aggressiveness (day 13)... Conference with Fabian's foster father, in the principal's presence... we discuss the damages... The father says I'm responsible, because I failed to prevent the escalation. He says: ›If the hotel guests are dissatisfied, the host gets replaced!‹ I... invite him... to see for himself... I raise the possibility of setting up an individual learning plan for Fabian, that we can supplement jointly with the father's inputs... A call from Max's mother. He has now been thoroughly tested by a psychologist. ›A ticking time bomb‹, was what she said. ›We'll be lucky if he only kills himself.‹ The psychologist advocates close child and adolescent psychiatry (day 17)... Conversation with Acatey's parents. Only the mother came... she knows it all by heart already... ›Why does Acatey act the way he does?‹... then she talks about the beatings that Acatey... received as a child... explanations, that have to do with an unwanted pregnancy... back then, in eastern Turkey... In any case, it was difficult to love the child... the father has no emotional connection to the son. ›Neither of us cares about him anymore‹, says the mother. ›We were in contact with a psychiatric clinic... Acatey did not want to talk with the psychiatrist. He said that the boy was filled with hate and violence, something needed to be done urgently. But we did not get a new appointment‹ (day 18)... Class open house evening... the parents read the subject roster on the wall... express agreement with the subjects I am emphasizing... Leon's mother says, her son has a big problem with being allowed to make mistakes. He had urgently to practice writing. He had been... covering up his weaknesses for years... During recess... a visit. The domestic partner of Leon's mother and a Hun friend, brass rings on his fingers, T-shirts with pit bull portraits. They came to see who is always beating up on Leon and to read the boys the riot act (day 28)... When I place a call to Jonas, loud Hip Hop music by a band greets me... A few days later, the phone line is disconnected... Acatey says, his parents had filed a grievance with the education office because he only gets nine hours of class (day 33)... Sent a list of all the unexcused absences by Jonas to the mother (day 72).«

The theme interprofessional work and relationship between school and community is represented at 4% in the journal. Interdisciplinary work occurs along lines like this: »Evening... phone conversation with Fabian's therapist... that Fabian acts almost ›submissive‹... in the three or four therapy sessions to date... and tries very hard to do what is asked of him. When it comes to school... he appropriates the victim role for himself. To the therapist, he selectively reports things that undergird this victim image (day 23).«

The school-community subject area is reflected in the following passages: »It is my birthday, and so I invite the students out to a Turkish pizzeria. When we get there, the door is still locked. Acatey beats with his fist against the glass. An old Turk runs over and tells him to knock it off... On the way back to school, a few boys get into an argument with the scaffolding crew on the church. Tim apparently had climbed up a ladder. I mediate. Then a group runs into the church... I herd the boys right away out of the church, after the experience at the cathedral (day 17)... The windows of an apartment across from the school are repeatedly broken with stones. Some of my students seem to know something. The principal has numerous conversations. The perpetrator is never identified (day 80).«

Acatey and Leon pose the biggest challenge for the teacher throughout, as attested to by the frequency with which these two names appear in the journal (Fig. 1.9). Acatey's (16) behavior is characterized by a high degree of rule breaking and violence. The boy's moods fluctuate in an unpredictable manner. Destructive impulses or merely movement impulses are acted out immediately. Acatey meets bonding overtures on the part of the teacher with suspicion and aggression. But slow, continuous progress emerges. As the youth begins to trust the teacher, he faces up to class assignments and endures the frustration he experiences due to his glaring learning deficits. Even if only in very small steps, he begins to slowly conform to the school system of rules, although there is occasional serious recidivism. Passing the moped exam on the one hand is an incentive for him to practice his reading and to learn more German. He also tentatively begins to let the teacher help him; however, he lacks discipline and perseverance. Some days, Acatey at least manages to concentrate for five or ten minutes. But then he jumps out of his chair, abandons his practice materials and obeys the most varied impulses.

Leon (15), newly enrolled at the school at the same time as the teacher took over the class, attaches himself closely to him. The teenager immediately takes the initiative to form a strong bond in which he at first feels protected and cared for. On this foundation, he engages in both a first reflexive examination of his own situation in life as well as the tentative reentry into school learning. Leon had completely ceased learning in the secondary school that he attended before. The pedagogical relationship between the teacher and Leon is put to a severe test after a few months when the boy not only steps out of the teacher's protective sphere, but suddenly switches to attacking his teacher for several weeks in an exceedingly destructive way. It may be assumed that the young man did this to be accepted by his classmates and admitted to the peer group he previously half dreaded. Once this phase ends, Leon is successful in resuming his reflexive examination of his own life situation and also his school learning in the previously developed form.

Fabian (16), the foster child, constantly avoids entering into a binding pedagogical relationship. His work habits remain erratic. Although he has the most intellectual potential in this study group, he steadfastly rejects learning and lets his impulses drive him in all directions. Fabian persists in his challenging behavior the entire time.

Max (14), abandoned by his abusive father, confronts the teacher in a suspicious, hostile manner and during the entire documented period cannot be motivated to enter into a trusting educational relationship. His pattern is one of provocation and attack. His emotional inner life seems torn, fear- and conflict-ridden so that all conversation about emotions and personal experience is blocked aggressively. He works at learning things in fits and starts as long as the group has no more than three or four students and the very dominant or impulsive ones are not in the room. Before the new teacher arrived at the school, Max stood on the ledge outside the window (4th floor) and threatened to jump.

Patrick's (16) behavior is gradually becoming more stable. He slowly gains confidence in his teacher, although, depending how he feels on a given day, he can also act highly aggressively and insultingly towards the teacher. In sheltered situations, where just a few and quieter classmates are present, he begins to grapple with his massive learning deficits and actually practices his reading and math. Wanting to pass the moped test spurs him on and he also accepts the teacher's help for it.

Dominik's (14) social behavior stabilizes soon after he also newly enrolled at the school. He quickly comes to trust the teacher, but also tends on occasion to behave in a provocative manner, probably to avoid jeopardizing his status among his peers. Initially, he applies himself well to his weekly and daily lesson plans, wavering now and then, but in the end continues to develop fairly well.

Tim (14), also newly enrolled at the school when the teacher arrived at the school, built a positive relationship with the teacher right from the start. Still, he repeatedly heaps verbal abuse on the teacher, but there is something playful and ritualistic about it and it evaporates quickly. Often, Tim smiles at the end of these swearing tirades and will say something conciliatory designed to mollify the teacher again. Similarly to Leon, in the beginning he attaches himself to the teacher but not nearly as closely. He quickly gains his footing in the new school environment. He abides by some rules; others he interprets loosely or circumvents.

Jonas (15) skips school completely after putting in a brief appearance at the start of the school year. After several attempts by the teacher to contact the parents about this, the telephone line was disconnected.

The social behavior of nearly all the students throughout this class made high demands on the teacher. Two students especially, Acatey and Leon, monopolize his attention (Fig. 1.9). Complicating the situation are the simultaneously prevailing learning problems of the 14-16 year old youths. As concerns students Leon, Patrick, Dominik and Tim, the teacher manages to create a reliable pedagogical relationship, based on which they can then reengage with the learning process. With Acatey this works only fitfully, with Max and Fabian hardly at all in the recorded time frame. The teacher continually offers an ongoing, reliable teaching relationship and exactly the same differentiated learning proposition. There is no deviating from them, even in turbulent times, as when Leon behaves in a very destructive manner toward the teacher. The differentiated and individualized learning opportunities in the form of daily and weekly lesson plans provide choices for the students, exerting a positive effect on the youths' willingness to learn. The teacher also provides numerous chances to participate in the lessons, also to address their own experience and backgrounds of experience and to express themselves. He praises and rewards positive student behavior in school. In Leon's case, he even succeeds in guiding the teenager to a deeper, reflexive examination of his educational biography and life circumstances. On the other hand, Jonas, the consistent school truant, drops off the teacher's radar. His name hardly appears any more in the journal.

This teacher is a »reflective practitioner« (Schön 1983) who seeks to understand what motivates his students' behavior. He analyzes the pedagogical and didactic processes so that he can better calibrate his own actions to the individual learning requirements of his students. On his own initiative, he consults with a coach outside the school in order to expand his own professional action palette.

A trusting relationship with parents and guardians is an important pillar of this school's culture. A close, stable working relationship marked by trust exists with Leon's mother and step father, as well as with the social workers in the group home where the teenager lives during the week. The whole of the work with respect to Leon is developed cooperatively and decisions are implemented consistently. The contacts with the respective parents of Max, Acatey, Patrick, Dominik and Tim are also under an auspicious sign. However, they do not agree on shared concepts for moving the teenagers ahead. Fabian's foster father initially met the teacher with mistrust and aggressiveness, but the teacher nonetheless manages to throw the switch leading to a more positive working relationship.

Cooperation with the police oriented toward intervention and prevention is not practiced for the school as a whole. There is also no collaboration between the school and companies, businesses or social institutions, such as churches, associations, etc. in the surrounding neighborhood. Systematic behavior control is not a component of this educational program. Still, a school-wide behavior management strategy emerges in which group constellations can be varied and changed within certain parameters and selected topics in problem behavior can be worked out situationally. A colleague also supports the teacher by taking Acatey along for hours at a time with her own students to play soccer or for moped training. From time to time, case discussions take place where the teacher can get inputs from his colleagues for further work with his students. In the daily course of things, the teacher must rely on himself.

This teacher, unfazed by extreme student behavior, proffers an educational relationship and differentiated learning opportunities. He works consistently on building up constructive and dismantling destructive student behavior. He is always trying to stimulate interest in learning on the part of students, develop individual learning goals jointly with the teenagers and to tailor appropriate learning materials to fit these highly individualized learning processes. Through individual coaching, this teacher could now be assisted in formulating his support goals relative to the individual students more clearly and to pursue them even more consistently afterwards. Acatey and Fabian urgently would need to be shown how to master their impulses so they can function in group settings. Max would need aid in coping with his fears so that he can put up with having other teenagers in the room. Given Tim's and Dominik's relatively stable personalities, they could be worked with more consistently in developing disciplined learning and work behavior. Dominik could also become a kind of peer tutor for Max. For Patrick, a consistent external learning environment would have to be created in which he would not have to hide his learning difficulties. Where sufficiently good contacts exist with the parents, but where there was as yet no sturdy working relationship, as in the case of Acatey, Fabian, Patrick and Tim, it seems that the problems and interests of the parents could be explored more extensively, in order to then involve them more intensively in the educational furtherance of their children. Where there is no contact at all, as with the mother of the truant Jonas, a joint home visit by the teacher and a youth services worker would seem to be indicated in order to make clear the scholastic interest in the youth's personal and professional future.

Based on these journal entries, interprofessional work is rather weakly developed. With respect to Leon, it actually works very well, because here the parents, home workers, youth services and teacher maintain steady contacts. The principal and the teacher corps should make it their goal to collaborate intensively outside the school with youth services, police, psychological, psychiatric and social pedagogical facilities. In this way, a truant like Jonas could eventually be reconnected to the school, and the criminal behavior of some of these students in the neighborhood could be curbed. That Acatey in the final analysis only gets about 5-6 hours classtime per week, though this is understandable in view of the stress he puts on the learning group, nevertheless, this kind of flexible but also truncated schooling gives rise to intervals without rules in which there are always new violations of boundaries and punishable acts and the youth becomes ever more alienated from school learning. An after-school program is lacking and should be urgently instituted in this school. Teacher support must be expanded; more presence and commitment by the principal could be helpful, as could involvement by the community surrounding the school. The bonding pedagogy practiced within this school is without doubt a great strength. Complementary behavior management would seem advisable, to further consolidate the behavior of individual students, protect fellow students, and to unburden the teacher with respect to his very high energy expenditure and to let him really teach. However, this would require working consistently, in an engaged and close manner, with all the extracurricular network partners, such as youth services, the police, and neighborhood stakeholders, etc. Of course, the school would need to have more personnel assigned, so that such a demanding learning group as described here can be consistently team-taught by two teachers.

It was not this teacher's intent to systematically treat categories derived from theory in his journal on a daily basis. He simply wanted to unburden his soul by writing down what he had experienced in his work (Fig. 1.10). This gives the textual content a high degree of subjective truth. He openly discusses the daily difficulties that confront him every day as teacher. A spontaneously authored journal text is naturally subjectively colored and does not allow for generalizations. To get as objective a picture of the educational work at this school as possible, we would need journals or verbal reflections from other teachers, the students, parents and the school principal. On the other hand, this journal gives us vivid insight into an educator's daily life that is very challenging. The journal only became available for scholarly evaluation after the fact, when the documented processes already were history. The teacher communicated verbally that he would have continued to put his pedagogical experiences to paper had a coach given him professional feedback on it. There might even be a chance that forms of student-related support planning, teacher coaching, pedagogical quality improvement and school enhancement in the field of teaching students with emotional and social difficulties in the future could rely in part on journals kept by teachers.

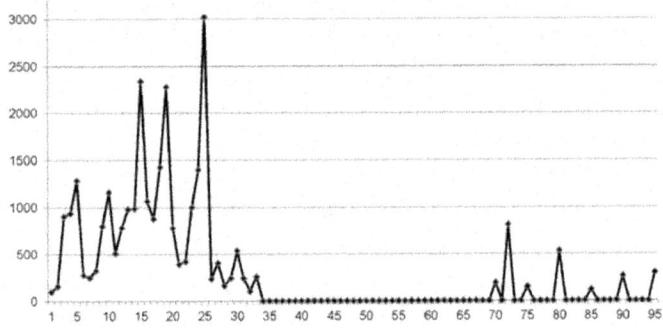

Figure 1.1: Quantity of written words per day

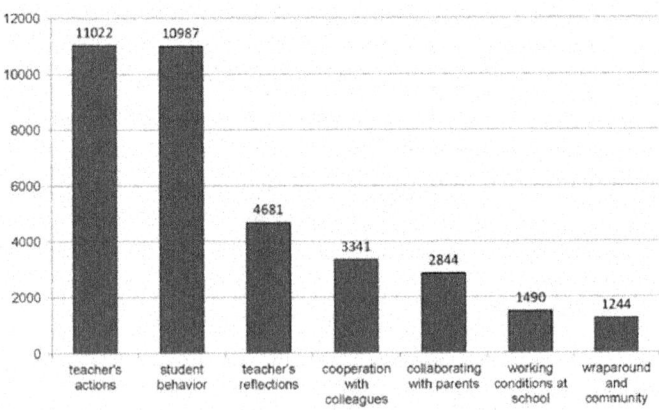

Figure 1.2: Themes of field notes and quantity of words in each category

Teaching on the Frontline | 37

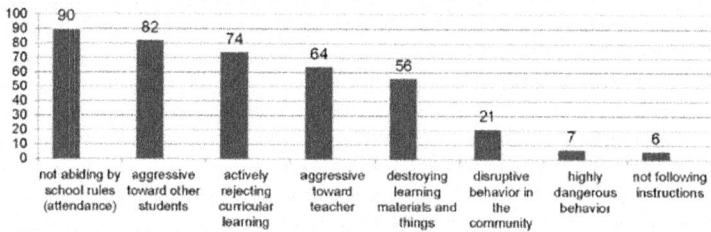

Figure 1.3: Student behavior: Negative patterns with quantity of words

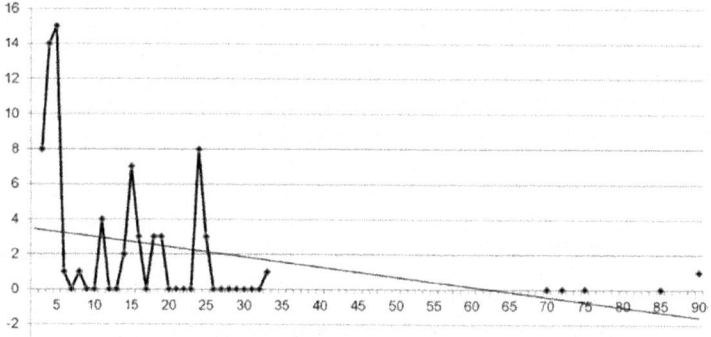

Figure 1.4: Students actively rejecting curricular learning with quantity of pattern per school day, and trend line

38 | Creating Learning Spaces

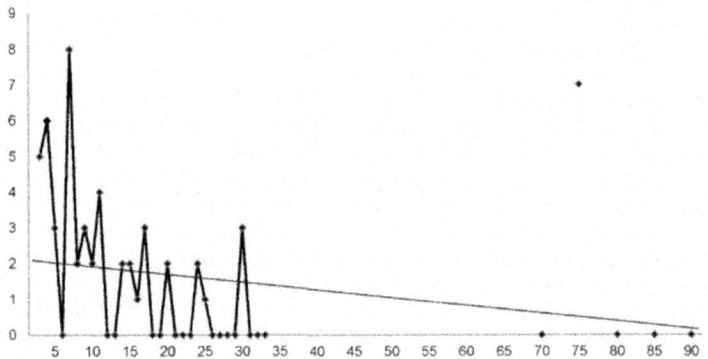

Figure 1.5: Students destroying learning materials and things with quantity of pattern per school day, and trend line

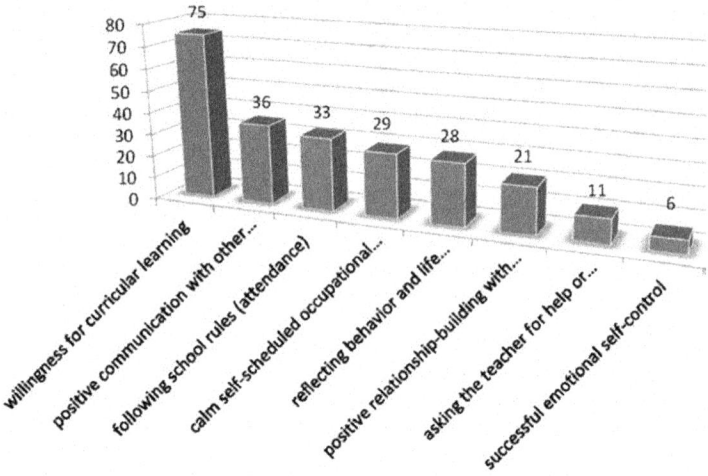

Figure 1.6: Student behavior: Positive patterns and quantity of pattern

Teaching on the Frontline | 39

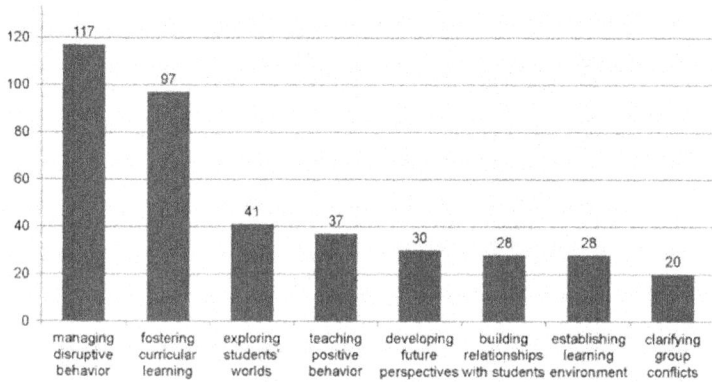

Figure 1.7: The teacher's actions: Patterns and quantity of pattern

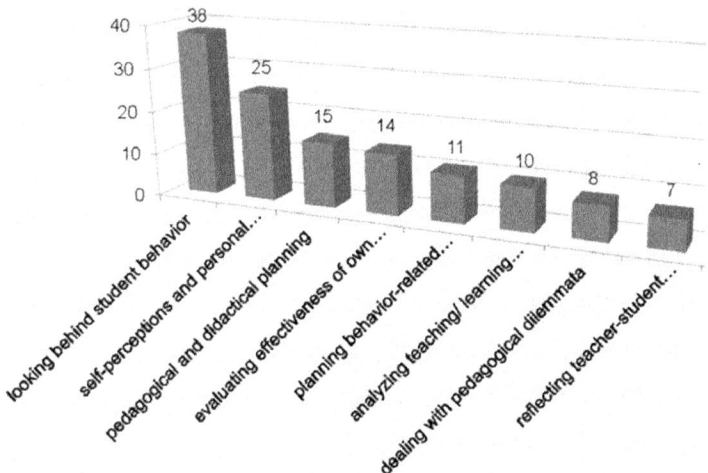

Figure 1.8: Patterns in the teacher's reflections and quantity of each pattern

40 | Creating Learning Spaces

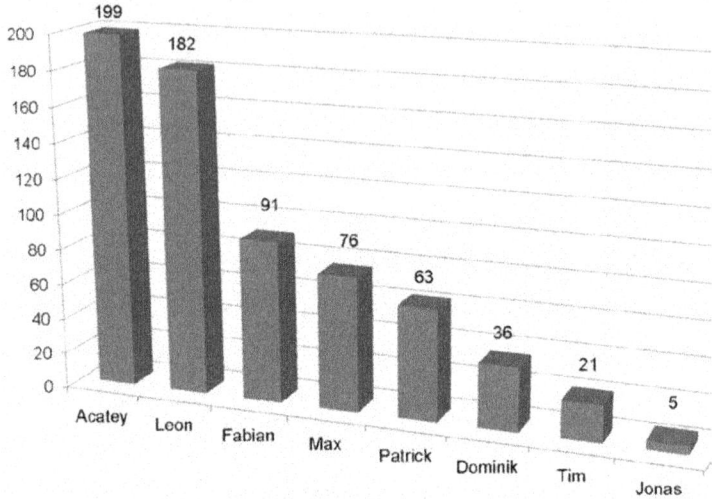

Figure 1.9: Frequency of individual students' names in the journal

Figure 1.10: The positive effects of journal writing in the context of teacher preparation and teacher training are well documented

2 Maladjusted Youth as Sand in the Gears?

Depending on the degree program, when I begin working with students of special education or inclusive education newly arrived at university, I read them a very specific story. It is a true story about something I experienced years ago as a public school teacher before I changed to the university full time. At the time, I was classroom teacher in a specialized school for children with emotional, social and behavioral difficulties and went on a one-week school trip, by train, that took us halfway across Germany, from the middle western part of the country up into the high north, a distance of about 650 km, right up to the Danish border. What follows below is an expanded version of the story that was published in abbreviated form at the time by a German newspaper and in a pedagogical journal (for a very short version see Broecher 2018).

The effectiveness of storytelling for getting a point across to people, for instance through »teaching stories« (Simmons 2006) or »scientific storytelling« (Gallagher 2011; Luna 2013; Petit et al., 2011) of course are already known. We can draw on approaches and studies that employ »storytelling as a pedagogical tool« (Abrahamson 1998) or deploy storytelling in work with students »to promote knowledge construction and learning« (Wiessner and Pfahl, 2007) especially in the area of higher education (e.g., Wallace and Gravells, 2010), teacher education (e.g., Grauer 2013, 2016) or school development (e.g., Griffiths et al., 2018).

The story »Incident on a Train« invariably moves the university students in a certain way. After the reading, usually a short silence reigns. However, then a lively discussion kicks off. It clearly reveals that this story not only calls on the emotions, but also mobilizes critical thinking on the subject of inclusion in school and society. The subject of inclusion in all its complexity suddenly becomes something real, specific, and tangible. It enables the students to identify the complicated mix of inclusionary and exclusionary forces at work in our German or European or Western-oriented society, to name it, to question it and to develop a perspective for deeper involvement in the subject, and think about the own attitudes, values and principles concerning the subject of inclusion, while being in a teacher education program (e.g., Avramidis and Norwich, 2002; Clarke and Drudy, 2006; Croll and Moses, 2000; Lawson et al., 2006; Moran 2007; Pecek and Macura-Milovanovic, 2012; Reynolds and Brown, 2010; Silverman 2007; Takala et al., 2012; Vanderfaeillie et al., 2003).

Before we proceed with reading the story, I want first to set the stage with three things, so that especially an international readership will have the necessary background for integrating that which took place. First: In Germany, as in many other countries, you can buy first class and second class train tickets. First class not only offers more comfort but also costs 50 percent more. Occasionally, it is also possible to book first class for a group at a price that beats the regular second class fare. Second: Westerland, the principal town on Sylt, is located in the island's midsection, right on the North Sea and can be reached directly by train that practically runs through the Wadden Sea over the »Hindenburgdamm« causeway that was built during the Weimar Republic. Third: By virtue of its location in the extreme northwest of Germany on the Atlantic, Sylt Island has an especially salubrious open ocean climate. This is why spa tourism developed there as early as the 19th century. The breathtakingly beautiful beaches and dunescapes attracted artists and intellectuals, but particularly the very well-to-do. Kampen on Sylt, with its picturesque thatch roofed houses, boasts Germany's highest-priced real estate. The boutiques there offer women's handbags or jackets for sale that would cost an elementary school teacher her entire month's salary. For the wealthy and the jet set, Sylt is an investment and status symbol. People from Germany's socially deprived areas could never in their lives hope to set foot on this marvelous island on their own. However, there is another Sylt and other ways of getting there. Several former military barracks located in the island's southern part were converted into school camps and youth hostels after World War II. That made it possible for large numbers of children and youth to come to Sylt regardless of their parents' sociocultural or socioeconomic situation, by going there on experiential pedagogy projects or school trips. So it was also for the group of nine- and ten-year old boys from a special school for children with emotional, social and behavioral difficulties at the center of our story.

This is not about the year when the only option for a train trip to Sylt I had left due to time constraints was to book a block of first class seats, because my colleague, who had joined me with his class, had needed so much time to get the money together that his girls and boys owed and when we then faced a situation on the return trip from Westerland to Cologne wherein society's well-heeled and pensioned sat in our seats in car 13, because car 14 had a problem with its electronics and so was off limits. First class, it seemed, was these ladies' and gentlemen's due, simply because, unlike us, they *were* first class. At first glance, it looked we seemed to be nothing more than social free-loaders, but fortunately we had valid tickets and demonstrable seat reservations. And so it came about that these kids from society's margin did wind up riding first class through Germany, in April of 2004, once I had negotiated emphatically with the well-heeled folks sitting in our seats, insisting that my students in fact got their seats – in first class. However, the story I really intended to tell dates back to sometime before that, to May of 1993. It, too, involves a class trip to Sylt, to Hörnum, to be exact, that picturesque town on the island's southern tip, where, if you clamber up the tallest dunes, you can see the ocean on both sides of the forty kilometers-long island – the foam-capped Atlantic to the west and the calmer Wadden Sea to the east. Some odd experiences transpired during the train trip there.

The smooth functioning of our railroads may be regarded as a symbol for reliability and well-planned forward progress. The train as emblem of social normality, functionality and productivity – however, only so long as no individuals board the train that are already sand in the gears and that can disrupt a train's steady progress or delay the train travelers from their business. Nonetheless, there are children and youth in this society that, by reason of their challenging behavior, are referred to special schools mostly because for deficits in emotional attachment and lack of an appropriate, supportive upbringing and education. There, with the help of a special pedagogy, they are to be brought back – reeducated, really – to the right way. After my colleague and I had attempted various influencing and fostering measures, with the involvement of the immediate school environment, on behalf of this band of *rascals*, a term I use humorously here, arrived the high point of the teaching program at that time: a one-week class trip to Sylt.

Our intent was for these kids, socialized by cell phone and computer, to be exposed to new experiences and insights in the fresh North Sea air, during group hikes along the beach and mudflats, on a boat trip to Hallig Hooge and the trotting of carriage horses on the Hallig. So it was that we found ourselves with that *unruly* troop of nine- and ten-year old boys once again riding on a train from Gummersbach in North Rhine Westphalia through Cologne to Westerland, in North Frisia, Schleswig-Holstein. They were ten in number this time, boys from a special school for children with emotional, social and behavioral difficulties. Each of them was like handling three of them when it came to rendering necessary supervision, care and attention. We took over several adjoining compartments. The month was May. It was a warm, sunny day full of anticipation for the beach life, North Sea air and fish rolls. Naturally, there was no way of keeping the boys in the compartments for more than half an hour. They obviously felt confined and within minutes already the first conflicts and squabbles started. They wanted out into the corridor. We put them off until later. They tried again and kept at it relentlessly. Finally, we let them out of the compartments. There simply was no other way. The boys ran up and down the car's corridor. Then some of them opened the windows. We closed the windows again and pointed out the potential dangers.

Soon after, I don't know how, the first few boys escaped into the neighboring open seating car. My colleague went in one direction and I myself in the other, to corral the boys again, while the social education teacher held down the fort outside the compartments. Breathing harder by the minute, I hurried through the corridors of the fully booked cars. Toward the front, I glimpsed a blond boy who belonged to our group; then he was gone. I ran a gauntlet of travel bags and sneakers that stuck out into the corridors. The glass doors hissed shut behind me. The trek through the cars seemed to me to take an eternity. Just before I reached the front of the train, it started to slow down. We entered the Bremen train station. The doors opened and out ran some of my students down the train platform toward the middle of the train; maybe they were looking for the Bremen Town Musicians? Was this then the result of the fairy tale projects that we had done in class? One of the boys cheekily stuck out his tongue at me through the train window. Then he took off, running along the train platform. A fun game. Hopefully, they would get back on the train in time, it pounded in my head. I longed for this day to end and wished myself into the counselor's room of the school hostel (»Fünf-Städte-Heim«), there to find solace in conversation with Mrs. Moll, a colleague from Cologne, over a cold Frisian beer. Mrs. Moll traveled to Hörnum with her classes every year around this time. All right, back the whole way. People began to notice me and regard me part sympathetically, part with annoyance and disquiet. Then, after a refreshment cart blocked my way and I somehow had managed to squeeze past it, out of breath I finally arrived back at the three compartments where I had started my futile chase after the students. In the meantime, the social education teacher had done a good job and gotten about half the runaways back into the compartments. Lastly, we corralled the remainder in the open seating car next to ours.

When the train had ground to a halt in Bremen, I made my way quickly along the platform toward the front to the engine and then systematically combed back through the train, to keep the boys from having any chance of escaping again. I happened straight onto a melee. One of the boys had jostled an elegantly-dressed woman having coffee. Her dress was covered with brown spots. Suddenly, there was a huge hue and cry, because an older man was pulling at the boy and cursing at him. I excused myself for the boy's behavior, pressed some Euros into the woman's hand for getting the dress cleaned, mumbled something about special children by way of more excuses and pushed the little group ahead of me and out of that car. It seemed to me that the entire train, regardless whether it was in first class or second class, had by now become affected by our ruckus-causing presence and was suffering because of it. My stress level kept rising. As the responsible classroom teacher, didn't I have to do a better job of keeping them in check? Was it a mistake after all to take troubled children like this on such a long trip? Instead of an eight hour train ride, perhaps I should have just taken them on a ten minute bus ride to the nearest youth hostel. I simply could not expect this well-set, well-heeled crowd, heading for their snug vacation houses, vacation apartments and hotel rooms in Westerland, Kampen or Keitum, to put up with something like this. On the other hand: Weren't we all somehow responsible for this young generation that, in some respects, had gone *off the track*? Could these people sitting here in the train, representing the larger society, simply avoid any responsibility? Could they just delegate it all to us special educators and social educators? Should they have peace and relaxation, at the cost of our energies being used up and having our nerves ruined? They wanted to travel, live, and lead a pleasant life. And us? Did we really deserve to be *sidetracked*? I read it in their accusing faces: »How could you travel with *these* children on *this* route to *this* destination?« Venomous looks castigated me. »Sylt, including the way to get there, belongs to *us*. Please stay home where you belong, in *your* socially deprived areas.«

No! Resentment suddenly welled up in me: »You are co-responsible for the social and cultural change process whose results and consequences I unfortunately have made it my job to suffer. From now on, feel free to experience some of the effects of your own politic or impolitic behavior, your lack of social engagement! I've had it with trying to shield you!« At a party recently a lawyer's wife had said to me, with a mixture of pity and incomprehension and a smug smile on her pursed lips, »Why on earth would you sacrifice yourself like that?«, as I was telling her about my work as special education teacher.

Fortunately, by now all boys were seated in the three compartments again. With the glass doors shut, both my colleagues and I stood in the corridor and assessed the situation. The sun shone brightly. We were drawing nearer to Hamburg. The train was barreling along. I listened to the loud, rhythmic clatter of the wheels. Satisfied, I looked in on the compartments in turn. To cheer them up, I had treated the boys to a round of Cokes. Lost in thought, they were sipping from the cans. I was glad that quiet had been restored. Only, it turned out to be a deceptive peace. In one of the compartments, the students had pulled down the orange colored sun shade. What I had failed to notice was that the window behind it had been pulled down all the way to the lowest stop. The train was hurtling along at top speed through the plain south of the Elbe.

Then, in an instant, it happened: The sun shade in that compartment was torn out the window, flapping wildly a few times and then the metal rod inserted at its bottom suddenly stabbed like a dagger from outside back in through the window panes doubled-up one behind the other. The rod remained firmly stuck in the glass. All around the puncture the glass was splintering. I immediately tore open the door. A warm blast of wind hit my face. Small glass fragments threatened to come loose from the Ping-Pong paddle-sized fracture. I pushed the boys out into the corridor as quickly as I could and locked the compartment door to prevent any harm to the children from flying glass splinters. I ventured in search of the conductor, to whom I described the situation. The uniformed man reacted with extreme irritation, even anger: »Can't you properly supervise your students?« We were nearly in Hamburg. The train had slowed and was already on the bridge across the Elbe. So, then the conductor phoned the chief conductor who decided to uncouple the car with the damaged window on safety grounds. This was done at the Hamburg-Dammtor train station. The passengers were told to detrain from the damaged car and to find another seat somewhere else on the train. The voices in the corridor and by the exits sounded angry. Suitcases were heaved about. Complaints rose about the lack of seats. Outside, on the station platform, furious looks came my way, mostly from men and women 55 years old and over, an embarrassing, reproachful and sometimes downright aggressive atmosphere. Finally, all of our charges were accommodated again in an open seat car at the tail end of the train. Thirty minutes behind schedule, the Intercity resumed its journey north. The students were nervous and agitated. My colleagues and I had our hands full trying to calm them down and to stabilize their behavior.

Suddenly, an incensed man rushed up to me, demanded my address and claimed damages for the train delay from me. It had caused him to miss an important business appointment in Westerland that, supposedly, involved millions. We had spoiled it for him. He would not stand for it. Sweat broke out on my forehead. I thought about my professional liability insurance. If worst came to worst... The other passengers in the open seating car listened intently. I didn't know how to react right away. I had just let myself fall exhausted into my new seat. Finally, stammering, I replied that it had not been my decision after all to uncouple the car because of the window damage. Of course, I also regretted the train's delay, but that was the chief conductor's decision. Snorting with rage, the man planted himself by my seat and repeated his demand.

But then the mood in the car, where many of the other relocated passengers had found seats, seemed to change. Suddenly, a group of women was standing in the aisle in support of me. »Look, can't you see what kind of work these young people are doing here? How would you like to be the one to do it? Come on, now! Do you really want to do this? What's this nonsense about millions? Stop it already. We've had it with your arrogant rudeness!« they went after the man. »Get lost, why don't you!« a woman called out to my accuser from further back. »The people from the special school have enough on their hands taking care of these kids!«

Irritated, the man who had harassed me mumbled something to himself, looked around nervously and finally went away. I was very grateful for the moral support that suddenly came my way from the fellow travelers, especially that group of women, all of them fiftyish. These women also gave us practical help by talking in a friendly way with the boys, paying attention and being considerate to them, responding to them and from time to time asking them how they were doing. This helped calm the boys down, and they started to relax. So, in this way, my colleagues and I received active support in looking after the students during the last segment from Hamburg-Dammtor to Westerland, which took the train another three hours. A pleasant warm feeling filled me. I started to relax, too. There was after all something like solidarity among this group of people rattling along on the rails, a common sense of responsibility. We were not alone. I also heard nothing more from the railroad (»Deutsche Bahn«) regarding this incident. Someone familiar with insurance matters told me that the railroad had largely replaced the metal rods inserted at the bottom of sun shades with plastic ones. Apparently, the metal rods had long been considered safety hazards. Late that evening in the counselors' room of the school camp in Hörnum, I told Mrs. Moll the whole story. As expected and hoped she, too, was there again. »That is why I always take the train with my classes«, she said, »because it gets me in touch with society.« I allowed myself a Frisian Pilsener. It had a nice, tangy taste.

The following are possible discussion questions for the students immediately following the story being told: Wherein resides the importance of this class trip for the children? What is the class teacher's experience and that of his two companions? What presumably is the perspective of the fellow passengers overall? What principles and societal forces does this businessman's behavior stand for? How would you advise the teacher to handle the businessman's demands? What significance did the behavior of the group of women toward the story's end have? What principles and societal forces do the women's actions represent? How would you personally have handled each of the situations? Was it a smart pedagogical decision to make such a long distance train trip with these students? Were the educational goals and the path embarked on in reasonable proportion? Later, as a teacher yourself, would you go on such a class trip with children with emotional, social and behavioral development needs? Was the problem aggravated by a student group coming from a separative school, which meant that *every* single boy had special emotional, social and behavioral needs and *no* children *without* such needs were along who might have served as role models or at least played a balancing role? What else spoke to you personally in the story? What else moved you? What does all this say about the current society and its relationship to the young generation? Do the narrated events contain a deeper truth or message? What conclusions can be drawn? In your view, how does all this apply to your studies now and later to your professional actions?

In the next stage, the story can be linked to the inclusion-theoretical discourse, because in this »incident on a train« the inclusive and exclusive forces of society are on display (cf. Woodward and Kohli, 2001). In the form of this real-life story from the educational workaday we receive a specific and emotionally-affecting description of »the dichotomy between in and out« (ibid., p. 2) as well as a description of the state of »how individuals are integrated into the social whole« (ibid., p. 4). These children are »both in and out of their society« (ibid., p. 9), »inclusion and exclusion are... in various ways intertwined« (ibid., p. 10). Further possible reference points for the academic discourse with the students are »equity in the social system« (Melucci 2001, p. 73), »education, citizenship and social justice« (e.g., Biesta et al., 2009; Birdwell et al., 2013; Mayo et al., 2009; McMurray and Niens, 2012; Tomlinson 2013), and »including students with behavioral difficulties in general education settings« (e.g., Goodman and Burton, 2010; MacFarlane and Marks Wolfson, 2013; Shearman 2003; Simpson 2004). »Social class« obviously has »effects on people's life chances« (Scott 2001, p. 143). The previous class trip episode also to Sylt that precedes the actual story (in which the teacher booked first class exclusively, but the children's places were at first taken away from them by the *actual* first class due to a technical problem in the next car) speaks volumes here.

How can educators contribute to »tackling inequality and exclusion« through »active citizenship and participation« (Machado and Vilrokx,

2001)? In this way, the connection between »education, equality and social cohesion« (Green et al., 2006) comes into focus, and with it »the role of education in promoting social cohesion« (ibid., p. 9), the question of »how education contributes toward civic engagement« (ibid., p. 19) and that we obviously require a »common sense of citizenship and values« (ibid., p. 30) if we are to foster social cohesion. These attitudes and values, which are what matters in all this, can be made concrete by an »ethics of belonging, care and obligation« (Macartney 2012) as well as by solidarity (Melucci 2001, pp. 74-77). The group of courageous and engaged women in the story demonstrates the importance and effectiveness of these action-guiding values for the creation of social cohesion by way of »community involvement« (Soresi et al., 2011). These women are always the sympathetic figures, the torchbearers of hope for a better social future, when discussing this story with university students.

My observations in university-level educational institutions and feedback from students indicate that seminars that are introduced and whose content is structured with this story have a particularly lasting effect on the students. It is exactly such an emotionally touching and affecting story from real educational life that can motivate students to explore the subject matter's complexity. Even many years later, students still have a lively recollection of the story »Incident on a Train«. It seems that they carry the events in this story with them as internal images. It is as if the future teachers have internalized those parts of this story that have potential for advancing social inclusion and social cohesion as an action model. It seems as if coming to terms with this story boosts the motivation for individual pedagogical engagement for more »social cohesion« and that this story helps students in special education as well as inclusive education to clarify even further their own action-oriented values in the sense of an »ethics of belonging and care« (Macartney 2012) and an »ethics of connectedness« (Frick and Frick, 2010).

52 | Creating Learning Spaces

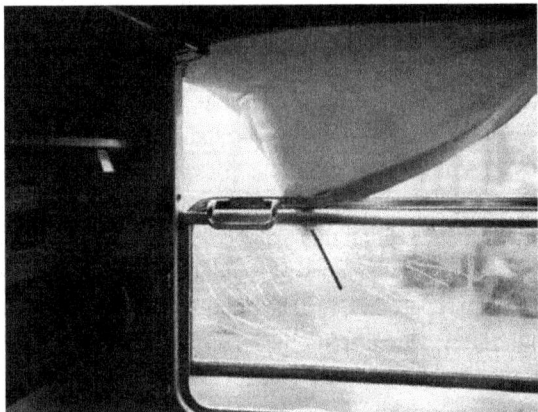

Figure 2.1

Incident on a train (photo: Angelika Schmachtenberg)

Figure 2.2

Shown here is the »Fünf-Städte-Heim«, a school-camp in Hörnum, located on the southern tip of the island of Sylt in the North Sea, between the foam-capped Atlantic Ocean to the west and the calmer Wadden Sea to the east. It was a place of special experiences, discoveries and encounters with school classes from other parts of Germany. The older parts of the buildings with their heavy wooden doors and wood floors date back to the Third Reich when troops were stationed here.

Maladjusted Youth as Sand in the Gears? | 53

Figures 2.3.-2.5

Teacher and students encounter each other in new and different ways in a unique landscape such as the one the Atlantic Ocean and the Wadden Sea offer here by the island of Sylt. Flying kites, digging canals with shovels, damming up water, we route and reroute it, only to realize that the movement of tides, the counter play of ebb and flood obey higher laws beyond man's power to modify. Rainer Lüders (Fig. 2.4) led generations of children and youth by the Wadden Sea and on the southern end of Sylt, including some of my own classes from alternative schools for students with emotional and behavioral difficulties. This teacher was an expert teller of tales and seaman's yarns. Holding out the prospect, say, of finding weapons dating from World War Two in the tidal flats, he motivated youngsters that scarcely ever walked any distance to set out on long hikes.

54 | Creating Learning Spaces

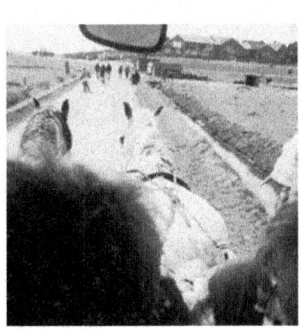

Figures 2.6 and 2.7

Children with emotional and behavioral difficulties experience the Wadden Sea biosphere with all their senses. Coming by ship from Sylt, they dock at Hallig Hooge and ride on horse-drawn carts to the individual dwelling mounds, rocked by the horses' slow trot along the way. The boys picture how the inhabitants of Hallig Hooge would bring themselves and their livestock to safety on the raised dwelling mounds and in their houses before an approaching storm tide. The boys would hang on the wagon driver's every word as he told the tale (Fig. 2.6).

Students sit in the little church in Keitum on Sylt during a class trip. It is about making contact with spiritual spheres in a raw landscape dominated by ocean and the wind. The children of contemporary society react in quite different ways to such a place. While the boy at left front in the picture retreats into himself and realizes that this church (in Keitum) from the late Middle Ages is a place for contemplation, the student in the middle of the church nave takes bodily possession of the place. In this second case, the pedagogic distance to be covered is considerably longer (Fig. 2.7)

3 Accessing Art with Movable Layout

In the research literature the positive effects of art making with regard to the emotional and social development of children and youth are well documented (e.g., Broecher 2012; Nissimov-Nahum 2008; Sandmire et al., 2012 etc.), also when youngsters experience some kind of social disintegration in their lives (e.g., Batsleer 2011; Gannon 2009; Prescott et al., 2008 etc.). But how can I teach art in a classroom with adolescent students who present emotional and social difficulties? When I look back on my 18 years as a teacher and school principal working with children and adolescents with social, emotional and behavioral difficulties in both specialized and inclusive settings and on my observational classroom research conducted at the juncture of art education and special education (e.g., Broecher 2000), it was primarily the students at the secondary school level, and especially those in specialized alternative settings, who frequently exhibited scarcely any spontaneous access to artistic forms like drawing, or painting. Some of these boys lacked confidence for drawing, others had little previous artistic knowledge or experience, or they dodged aesthetic-creative assignments entirely.

Many of these students had lost the spontaneous childlike delight in pictorial storytelling and self-expression or, in some cases, depending on the individual socialization background, it seemed they had never known it at all. Rather than putting something on paper that did not measure up to their own inflated expectations derived from media models, they chose not to make any picture at all and refused to cooperate in class. Already a problem that is encountered in this age group generally, it was that much more pronounced in students with emotional and social difficulties and posed extreme challenges for me as a teacher who wanted, and was obligated, to make art with this audience.

To deal productively with this situation and get these youngsters to make pictures anyway, over the years I developed a kind of Movable Layout, in essence a collage-assisted drawing technique. For this purpose, I took availed myself of a series of pedagogic and education precepts whose effectiveness research had confirmed, i.e., breaking up the task components, explicit and direct instruction, choice-making, and opportunities to respond. With this research-based technique, students with emotional and social needs, who often exhibit difficulties with pictorial exposition or who completely refuse to draw because of the fear of failure, can easily be guided into the artistic terrain and encouraged to have fun producing pictures on their own, never mind any obvious difficulties. The academic intervention undertaken in this way also turns out to be a behavioral intervention.

The consensus in research holds that emotional and behavioral difficulties go hand in hand with academic learning difficulties. Students with emotional and social needs often show large academic achievement deficits across all content areas (Nelson et al., 2004). »A key finding in the literature is that EBD students usually struggle academically« (Nicholson 2014, p. 180). They disrupt their own learning and the learning of others (Trout et al., 2003, Reid et al., 2004), although the interplay of both variables is very intricate and not yet fully understood (Algozzine et al., 2011). So do we start with *learning* or with *behavior* – or both? There is a »line of thinking« in the theory that »pre-supposes that academic instruction cannot take place unless a student's behavior is first under control« (Wehby et al., 2003, p. 195). This can be contrasted with the high impact of academic instruction that is effective from the outset, albeit accompanied and supported by behavioral interventions.

Hence, as my many years of application in the field have also convinced me, we need to acknowledge the important role played by academic instruction on which we can then build effective academic, social

Accessing Art with Movable Layout | 57

and behavioral learning. Much of the off-task behavior of students with emotional and social difficulties is escape-maintained. Academic failure and escape-motivated problem-behavior are functionally related and consequently academic interventions can be considered as a meaningful treatment response. In other words: when we want to reduce problem- and off-task behaviors and increase on-task behaviors, research suggests instructional adaptations are effective interventions (Lee et al., 1999, p. 196).

The object therefore is to carry out an »instructional adaptation« that is linked to the goal of more effective management of »escape-maintained behavior« in the classroom (Moore et al., 2005). The »curricular expectations« that apply to a specific classroom subject are »antecedent events« and when these are »mismatched with current student skill levels«, undesirable classroom behavior may be the consequence (ibid., p. 216). Consequently, what is mainly needed is to ensure an »appropriate instructional match between curriculum (and/or instructional materials and methods) and the existing level of student academic skills« (ibid., p. 217). The instructional adaptations will function as pro-active interventions because they often change the learning situations that trigger the problem behavior and ameliorate them for students with emotional and behavioral difficulties (Lee et al.,1999, p. 196). Such an alternative will now be presented and analyzed specifically for teaching art in a challenging classroom.

However, this is not merely about reducing the task load. What it does call for is a special way of structuring the problem presentation and ways of solving it. To simply make tasks easier would undermine the curricular educational requirements for students with emotional and behavioral difficulties and also not challenge the students enough so they can develop. What the students need much more is stimuli for learning, they need »opportunities to acquire new skills and expand their behavioral repertoires« (Moore et al., 2005, p. 217). That is why breaking up the task components, splitting up the workload into steps, and adapting the task so that the respective steps are of shorter duration is crucial.

These strategies lead to more on-task behavior (Nicholson 2014, pp. 183-184).

Tightly tied into this is the teaching of component skills. The term »component skills« refers to »lower-level skills that collectively make up complex higher level skills«. When one or more component skills are lacking, students fail to learn the complex skill. But if the students »possess all component skills necessary to learn a task, learning the larger task is easier and access to positive reinforcement is increased« (Lee et al., 1999, p. 196).

In classroom work with the Movable Layout, the first thing that happens is a simplification of the perspectival and compositional relationships and demands. Given the chance to arrange the figure elements against a background initially on a trial basis (Fig. 3.1), then to manipulate them in new and different ways, makes perspective and the pictorial space concrete for the student as foreground-background, in front of-behind, etc. and dynamically tangible, comprehensible and adjustable. In addition, teacher input can help students understand this step better and complete it successfully.

Combined with the principle of substitution for missing or incomplete cognitive figurative representations, depending on an adolescent's individual learning level, previous aesthetic socialization and learning biography, this reduction of complexity on the formal level of the perspectival picture composition corresponds with a high degree of complexity of visual narrative and visual message on the content level. By using this method, the student is guided step by step to a pictorial creation that is in most cases very satisfying for him.

The second factor by which the Movable Layout also contributes to academic learning and behavior improvement lies in the way it integrates explicit or direct instructional practices. Explicit instruction is understood here as an »unambiguous and direct approach to teaching, with an emphasis on providing students clear statements about what is to be learned, proceeding in small steps with concrete and varied examples, checking for student understanding, and achieving active and successful student participation« (Nelson et al., 2014, p. 363). The key elements or functions relating to explicit or direct instruction are: »1. Daily review and prerequisite skill check, 2. Teaching of new content, 3. Guided practice, 4. Independent practice, 5. Weekly and monthly reviews« (ibid., pp. 367-374). Using direct instruction, as described by Eisner Hirsch et al. (2014, p. 209), means »limit the amount of material students receive at one time, give clear and detailed instructions and explanations, guide students as they begin to practice«. This hands-on approach as part of a highly structured pedagogic framework lets the students learn how to work step by step with the Movable Layout and the subsequent variations it makes possible.

Third, the Movable Layout despite, or perhaps because of, its high degree of pre-structuring, allows the students with emotional, social, and behavioral difficulties choice-making in various ways. The positive effects of choice-making as interventions that reduce problem behavior are accepted as givens in research (Green et al., 2011; Shogren et al., 2004). The more confrontational, the more disruptive a student's behavior is, the more important and effective choice-making is as an entry to a productive learning process. The closer we approach positive, on-task student behavior on the other hand, as in general education settings, the sooner choice-making also could and should be dispensed with in order to achieve an optimum level of academic learning (Mizener and Williams, 2009). Movable Layout, however, was specifically developed for adolescents with very disrupted behavior patterns, such as those encountered in specialized settings in alternative schools or in the Tier III area of a school-wide model.

Here choice-making, in conjunction with other precepts, for example, breaking up the task components as well as explicit or direct instructional practices, is of fundamental importance for dismantling learning resistances in adolescents. In this, different types of choice-making can come into play for students with emotional and social difficulties, from preference and choice of activity (Romaniuk and Miltenberger, 2001), through within-activity choices (Cole and Levinson, 2002) to a choice of task sequences (Kern et al., 2001). With Movable Layout, the youngsters can choose from many different picture backgrounds and picture elements, as provided for in specific lesson plans. Depending on circumstances, they may also freely choose the subject of their art work, or I may give them a choice of two ready-made, combined background-and-figure sets. Next they have the opportunity to choose the materials and artistic technique for doing further work on a copy of their pictorial composition.

Fourth, classroom work with the Movable Layout includes a variety of opportunities to respond (OTR), understood as instructive stimuli that occasion the student responses (Haydon et al., 2012; Sutherland et al., 2003). We need to take into account that higher rates of OTRs are associated with increased on-task behavior and decreased disruptive behavior (Sutherland and Wehby, 2001) and also be clear in connection with the Movable Layout, that besides »teacher-directed individual responding«, »production responses« (Haydon et al., p. 24) are a given, particularly in the creative processes themselves. In this way, the Movable Layout gives every individual student a chance to tell a story using pictures to share about himself and the world of his thoughts and lived life and, beyond that, to communicate verbally, either in conversation with the teacher and/or the other students.

On the content level, thanks to the tools provided, offered now is the possibility of a complex, many-layered and detailed picture message or picture story. The students get the opportunity to communicate in an artistically sound manner and at the same time to present an altogether respectable whole artistic composition. This means that the youngsters now are able to express considerably more pictorially than they could using just their intrinsic artistic abilities. With the Movable Layout system they step up to complex picture composition and spatial organization that is capable of meeting their own demands far more than might a free-hand drawing or a free-hand pictorial design. Thus, problems and fears about artistic expression are circumvented and then dismantled step by step through repetition of successful picture making experiences. The build-up of frustrations or aggressions, which often lead to the artistic activity being dropped or not even begun in the first place, ceases to be a problem.

The outcome is quiet, disciplined creative activity, enjoyable pictorial experimentation and a gradual expansion of native drawing and design abilities. This in turn has a positive effect on learning motivation and the learning and working behavior of a youngster with emotional and social difficulties. When this happens, it is recommended to consolidate and further promote positive developments in the area of student behavior with behavior-specific praise on the teacher's part (e.g., Kalis et al., 2007; Marchant and Anderson, 2012; Partin et al., 2010).

Particularly in teaching creative arts, a task may have »other aversive properties« than just the level of difficulty (Moore et al., 2005, p. 217). Boys from problematic socioeconomic communities – in the field of educating students with emotional, social, and behavioral difficulties, after all, we deal primarily with boys – may perform masculinities that not only are hostile to school learning in general but can also produce resistance vis à vis participation in the creative arts, since they are perceived as falling more into the female sphere because the expression of emotions is associated with them. Boys who grow up in environments with more conventional male gender roles constructions expose themselves in their school peer group to a high risk of having their masculinity questioned and of being bullied when they engage in the creative arts (Scholes and Nagel, 2012).

This can have very negative consequences for the boys affected because, due to these constraints and restrictions, they miss out on acquiring the necessary skills that they actually need to play an active, productive role and earn a living in the »creative economy« (ibid., p. 980) that has supplanted the industrial age. To address these kinds of difficulties productively and to ensure that young people from such problem backgrounds accept classroom work with Movable Layouts, the technical and rational-seeming aspects of this method are emphasized up front.

Even if life topics are likely to be addressed directly or indirectly in the pictures, it is recommended that these be acknowledged in this early phase but not dwelled on as subject for discussion. Only when a greater degree of behavioral confidence is attained with students with emotional and social difficulties, and develops in parallel with successes in the field of academic learning, can I, as a teacher, carefully begin to address the picture *contents* and thus possibly also begin making the contents of a student's special life experience a subject of discussion. But to begin with, discussed only are perspectival issues, overlaps, size proportions, contrasts, drawing techniques, printing techniques, possibilities of computer image processing, etc. This is safe ground for all participants, students as well as teachers.

The idea of placing individual figurative elements on a background, to move them around until a desired effect is achieved and then to photocopy the final arrangement and then continue to work on it is basic graphics technique. Movable Layout is a system of manipulable picture backgrounds and elements. To make working with this method possible, the first thing to do is assemble a basic assortment of pictorial elements and backgrounds, for instance, by copying drawings by famous artists, figures from how-to-draw books, and the like. Many documents can furnish details that can be enlarged or reduced or otherwise adjusted with image editing software. The elements are then printed and or cut out. The picture backgrounds are mounted or laminated on poster board to make them more durable. Among the image backgrounds the following might be found: Gentle hills rising out of fog, as well as dense forests or barren, craggy rocks in an otherwise empty appearing landscape. On some of the backgrounds I have used white-out to delete central figures, animals etc. from the printed graphics. I have views of villages, which can stimulate both representations of idylls and tranquility but also boredom and sadness.

Some background scenes I keep deliberately very amorphous and indistinct, specially processed in part to leave as much room for imagination as possible. They virtually invite the projection of subjective imaginings onto them. The city scenes show tidy avenues as well as street canyons, apartment blocks and dark subway shafts. There are also house or apartment interiors, e.g., a kitchen with dining table, living room with sofa, home office, teenagers' rooms, bedrooms; in short, rooms where a relevant event or imaginative content can be staged. The set of varied pictorial elements should span a broad spectrum from the aspects of content and motifs.

I derive the selection criteria from my knowledge of the age-specific interests of the learning groups that I work with. Accordingly, I compile my ensemble in different ways depending on age but also the youngsters' life themes and conflict burdens, severity of social backgrounds and emotional experiences. The repertoire of figure cutouts can be made up of pictures of men, women, children, adolescents, parent-child groupings, and so on. They can be trimmed with scissors before being placed into the picture to achieve an optimal fit with what the student personally intends to depict. Further, there are pictures of bicycles, motorcycles, cars, trucks, trains, planes, carriages, furniture, houses, animals and all sorts of implements and furnishings, from the living room chair all the way to the toothbrush. Acquiring some light, easy to carry cases is highly recommended. One case can hold as many as 150 of the background images mounted or laminated on poster board.

The other case is dedicated to the movable figures. By continually adding to the collection over the years, newly copying or printing out damaged items and in between constantly making a few copies, enlarging, or shrinking drawing elements that you come across out and make their way into the case, within a few years it is easy to accumulate 6,000 to 8,000 elements. With this collection it is possible to work cogently and in a richly varied manner. But to start with, I will only have a much smaller collection that I gradually build up. Occasionally, the students will also help to cut out newly copied picture elements. To enhance the chances of finding suitable motifs and elements, the students themselves also get to choose images from art books, catalogs, other printed images or the Internet. They copy, enlarge, or shrink them and then add these supplementary, found elements to their own compositions and then enhance them by drawing on them.

When I present too many mixed-up elements to a given study group, it may be asking too much from the individual students in the way of sensory overload. I therefore went on to set up folders arranged by element subject matter, for instance, by images of children, adolescents, adults, wild animals, domestic animals, buildings or vehicles. It also lets me hand the students just the folder with child figures and animals and specify the topic as »An experience with an animal.«

I started out with backgrounds in the DIN A3 format, but I soon noticed that many youngsters later found it difficult to artistically enhance the entire picture surface. The area simply looked too large to them. They lacked the endurance. As a complementary alternative, I therefore put together a smaller set of backgrounds reduced to DIN A4. From then on, I let some students decide for themselves whether they wanted to work with a smaller or a larger format, making another instance of choice-making a part of this process.

When students first start working with the Movable Layout system, I recommend not posing a topic at the start. Usually the motivation is strong enough without it, i.e., they very eagerly search through the picture elements, try them, arrange them, so that at the early juncture, they would hardly pay attention to a subject assigned. Later on, it may be useful to offer something along the following lines: »A weekend at my house«, »Something that happened here in the school«, »Recently something strange happened to me«, »On the go with my friends«, etc. Through these and similar topics, the students receive stimuli as well as basic ideas through which a pictorial exploration of an experiential content can be achieved. »When I really got upset at school« could also be a topic on the basis of which it would be possible to work on emotional or social issues with students that are already exhibiting more stable behavior.

In the creative process, a series of operations play a special role, the first of which consists of ordering, experimenting and arranging. The creative process unwinds in a similar manner regardless if the assignment is free-form without subject or tied to a specific topic: First, the youngsters select a background, followed by a series of drawing elements. They arrange, experiment, move, latch on to an idea or discard it. They move pictorial elements, e.g, furniture, animals, people, etc. back and forth across the chosen background until they arrive at a pleasing arrangement. It happens from time to time that a student, in follow up to this introductory experience, desires to change the background to a different one from the one chosen initially. I advise making this an option.

It has also happened to me that a student would rather design an entire background on his own against which to position the prepared picture elements. This type of initiative taking should be supported anytime, with the rule of thumb being: »As many rules and pre-structuring by the teacher as necessary, as much independent creativity by the students as possible.« Anyone not needing the Movable Layout who would rather work free-hand should be allowed to do it! The method is designed as an aid in independent composition and should therefore not be experienced as confining. But cases like this are the exception to the rule.

Next is selecting and then attaching the picture elements, followed by photocopying the layout. The loose elements are attached with small strips of double-sided adhesive masking tape and one or more photocopies are made of the prepared layout. These copies are then enhanced using various artistic methods. The image backgrounds and moving elements are reusable and find their way back into the cases or folders. When enhancing the copied composition with artistic means, one possibility for further creative work on the picture is to complete drawing it or adding drawings.

Students who have learning problems or learning disabilities in particular usually begin by coloring in their pictures or over them with felt tip markers. Variations here might consist of offering the children and teenagers crayons, oil pastels or water colors. Even just coloring as an entry into a higher artistic compositional process is worthwhile, because the almost always handsome and brilliantly colored resulting pictures give satisfaction to the students who are often accustomed to failure; they fill them with pride and so motivate them to go on. In my experience, youngsters with behavioral problems especially like working with black felt tip pens. Wherever possible, I encourage the students to draw in missing shape parts or simple lines, extend them or to add entirely new details to the pictures by drawing them in.

Another possibility for artistically enhancing the copies besides drawing with felt-tip pen, pencil, fountain pen or nib is painting on them with brush and opaque colors to the point where the contours of the graphic elements are covered to the extent possible, perhaps gradually becoming completely invisible (Fig. 3.3). Other artistic options are to be found in transforming, experimenting and abstracting. Based on many years of observation, students with behavior problems – as opposed to those with severe learning difficulties – tend to do more spontaneous drawing on the copied compositions and so transform the content. Transformation to some extent corresponds to their natural tendency, a circumstance that can be honored as thoroughly positive in this context, for this natural tendency to transformation that numerous students with emotional and social evidence here is put in the service of artistic work.

Impressively original results can be achieved with the help of monotype or flat screen printing (Fig. 3.4). In this process, sheets of plexiglass (real glass is not used for safety reasons), have a thick coat of water-soluble ink rolled onto them. The layout copy with the picture side facing up is deposited lightly on the inked surface and then the contours of the landscape, houses, people, or animals are traced firmly with a pencil so that they are pressed into the ink. The sheet can also be placed step-wise on differently colored plates. Once again, the image produced by the monotype can be painted on by dissolving the water-based remaining paint for a clouded or fogged appearance or adding a new color accent. To encourage such experiments and playfulness, it is best to make several copies of the previously created template. In addition, several computer-based image processing applications offer the ability to twist scanned-in compositions, to distort, manipulate and change them by using various filters. The resulting images can once more be painted or drawn on, both on the computer screen and also on a paper print (Fig. 3.2). The picture versions can also be cut up and assembled in new or different ways.

Also, experiments on the copy machine or on a scanner can be done by turning the template during the exposure process or pulling it out sideways. This produces abstraction and distortion effects. Depending on which direction you pull the sheet, it results in stretching or compressions, twisting of figures, buildings, etc. From these copies, complete new pictorial compositions can be collaged and overpainted again. In this way, an increasing degree of freedom is experienced in handling the original design. Another alternative is creating a short picture story or sequence of pictures from several individual pictures, as in a comic strip. It need only have the same characters and elements differently arranged from scene to scene and each time it is copied or scanned, then varied and combined into a story.

It is also conceivable that a certain composition is varied in different ways. This can lead to staging a kind of symbolic trial action or also creative action on the picture level that could also play a role later on in helping the young people deal with real-world tasks confronting them.

Multiple references to the world of art are given. The history of art is filled with examples of pictures, which can be used by way of introduction, concurrently, in conclusion or in comparison, etc. The topics of abstraction, working in series, or confrontation with art works already pose markedly higher intellectual demands on the students. For many of them, this is unfamiliar territory, but the Movable Layout with its rich set of variations provides an orientation that also gives youngsters with emotional and social difficulties the confidence to explore this terrain step by step.

The method can be used in different teaching contexts. Hence, I successfully made the technique the focus of a teacher-guided series of classes and systematically worked through the MLT steps and variable possibilities with the students in a formal course. This method is useful, for example, when I teach art as subject teacher to a specialized class for two hours per week. It works similarly in an inclusive setting, where I mostly work in a class as a part-time co-teacher. As a class teacher in a school I also have the option of making available to my students the picture backgrounds and picture elements over several weeks during specific class hours as part of course offerings under daily and weekly lesson plans. The Movable Layout system here is part of a broader overall palette of curricular offerings which the students can choose from.

The first phase of choosing and arranging of picture elements is easier when done with the study group as a whole. It requires the use of all available tables for two hours on which to spread all the material. I think it is advisable to do further enhancement work in more open learning processes. In this way, more opportunities are provided for individual guidance discussions with the students. It is also a fact that not all students show the same degree of perseverance when it comes to working on the pictures. The first phase of choosing and arranging usually proceeds in a highly motivated way. When faced with a copy of their own composition, it already starts to look more like *work*. Some students, particularly those with severe behavioral problems, often only color the pictures very cursorily or in a fragmentary way or soon break off their artistic activity again. The parallel installation of other learning stations with different contents and methods allows these learners to easily switch from one activity to another and relieves me of the pressure of having to make the students continue working against their will or forcing me to come up immediately in that situation with an alternative way of occupying those still unsettled, hurried, impatient learners. Often, after ten or twenty minutes doing arithmetic on the computer, they return to their picture to continue working on it for a while. In this connection, too, choice-making is operating as a fundamental pedagogical principle.

The Movable Layout allows the construction of complex visual narratives, so the chance to discuss the students' compositions should definitely be grasped. There are opportunities to respond on several levels here, through conversation but also in the form of mini essays. During inclusive instruction in primary schools, I have usually let the whole class write stories about their finished pictures. In classes with up to thirty children, this is often the only way to get to hear something from everyone and to learn. Depending on the specific setting, the texts can be read in small groups and discussed. I gave special support to the groups of students with emotional and social difficulties, so that an active participation by all and a constructive working atmosphere in working with the pictures and self-written stories prevailed. For students that have concurrent learning problems, it is often useful to specify beginning sentences fragments that they then complete or to let the youngsters talk about their pictures while I record them. The text that I write down and then type up I hand back to the student to read, add to and develop further. Fundamental here is assessing the written expression skills carefully case by case to avoid provoking any refusal reactions stemming from negative expectations regarding success.

Even students who initially very much shrink from aesthetic-creative tasks or learning opportunities or reject them vehemently – be it because of the task's high complexity and the resulting expectations of failure or because of unsettling gender identity issues that are associated with art – unexpectedly find themselves in a complex process of designing, experimenting and composing thanks to the Movable Layout Technique. In this way, escape-maintained disruptive student behavior can be circumvented, by substituting missing artistic potential and, when it comes to the process of creating pictures, by reducing the complexity of pictorial composition and segmenting it into steps that the boys are capable of mastering. By employing this method, work interruptions triggered by frustration can be avoided. Students with serious artistic difficulties or refusal attitudes are easily and successfully guided into the artistic terrain and encouraged to independently lay out pictures and creative compositions in a fun way. It opens up ways to freer forms of artistic work.

A few years ago I started publishing the first texts and picture volumes on the Movable Layout Technique in German art education and special education journals. I also put on classes and seminars to teach MLT in connection with pre-service teacher education in the field of special education and inclusive education at the University of Cologne and in connection with in-service teacher trainings. What is recorded here is based on 18 years of observational classroom research that I have conducted as a teacher-researcher in specialized and inclusive settings, as well as in the transition region.

The Movable Layout Technique is based on evidence-based precepts such as breaking up the task components, explicit and direct instruction, choice-making, and opportunities to respond and, in view of the mostly male adolescents in the field, it is gender-sensitive by moving the more technical aspects of the method to the fore. In this respect, the Movable Layout, even if it has not yet been subjected to systematic empirical testing, can still be regarded as *research-based* since it employs evidence-based practices that are applied guided by theory to the field of art education in connection with pedagogy and didactics.

My many years of classroom observations suggest the suitability and effectiveness of the Movable Layout Technique in the fields of special and inclusive education. This holds particularly true for those young men who behave in a highly disruptive way, who consequently are on Tier III of a school-wide model or in separate, specialized school environments. Because they have additional, considerable learning deficits and learning difficulties due to their special educational biography, because they may reject art as a problematic, their own masculine identity-threatening, gender issue, they have almost completely dropped out of artistic production or completely refuse it in the school context. A systematic, empirical investigation in the near future of the method in this pedagogical-educational connection would seem to be meaningful and worthwhile, in order to explore in still more depth opportunities and educational potentials inherent in Movable Layout Technique.

Accessing Art with Movable Layout | 71

Figures 3.1 and 3.2

72 | Creating Learning Spaces

Figures 3.3 and 3.4

4 Challenging Disabling School Policies

Since 2003, the »Training Room Program (TRP)«, a time-out model that is based on the American »Responsible Thinking Process (RTP)«, has become established in German schools in response to students' increasingly challenging learning and social behavior. School administrators and academics alike recommend the implementation of the TRP as part of their efforts to conform to the UN convention in order to ensure the success of inclusive schooling for students with emotional and social needs. But in doing so, formal inclusion and temporary exclusion within the school become interconnected.

The results yielded by this program evaluation show that there is to date no convincing empirical evidence as to the effectiveness of the TRP. On the contrary, the data indicate that the TRP actually has a negative impact on teaching and learning processes and on the culture of the school as a whole. While the TRP aims to enhance levels of classroom discipline and relieve pressure on the teacher, the program simultaneously impedes the development of a participative and empowering learning culture, even though it is precisely this factor which is indispensable for the successful inclusion of learners with emotional and social needs. The TRP's educational ideals and its conception of human beings are also a serious cause for concern. The conclusion outlines alternative concepts which are more suitable for the provision of inclusive schooling for students with emotional and social needs.

In Germany, the »Training Room Program (TRP)«, first emerged shortly after the turn of the century. It was Balke (2003), Bründel and Simon (2003, 2007, 2013) and Claßen and Nießen (2006), whose publications and internet pages first introduced the program into the practice of school teaching, together with the teacher training programs for which it provided a base. The theoretical roots of the TRP are embedded in the »Responsible Thinking Process (RTP)« developed in the USA by Ford (2004), a program which in turn was based on control theory (Powers 1998; Marken 2002).

It is difficult to accurately estimate the number of German schools which are working with the program. In North Rhine-Westphalia, 142 secondary schools were working with the TRP when Balz (2004) conducted his survey. If we extrapolate this number to the total number of schools in this Bundesland (N=2.740), then the result is 5.2%. Recent statistics are not available from the other 15 Bundesländer. Interviews with local education authorities together with research undertaken on the internet would appear to support the estimate that approximately 10%-15% of all German schools, according to region, are working with the TRP. Some schools work with the TRP, but do not make this information externally available. The TRP is also used to some degree in modified forms and under different names (e.g., »Island Room«).

The stated aim of the TRP is to instill discipline in the classroom, thereby enabling lessons to take place *without interruption*. The TRP is based on the following principles: »Every teacher has the right to teach without interruption whilst at the same time bearing the responsibility for providing high-quality classes. Every student is entitled to high-quality classes whilst at the same time ensuring that classes can proceed without interruption. Teachers and students must show respect for their mutual rights and shoulder their respective responsibilities« (Bründel and Simon, 2003, p. 38). If a student fails to abide by these rules, the teacher can ask the student to leave the classroom and go to the training room. The teacher decides when the student should leave.

Before this happens, the teacher will ask the student if he is prepared to cease his disruptive behavior. Depending on his answer, the student will be allowed to remain in the classroom or will decide to go to the training room. In the training room, a teacher or social worker will be waiting for the student and will call upon him/her to reflect self-critically upon his/her disruptive behavior. During this process he must acknowledge e.g. the following: »What did I do? I annoyed my teacher. I ran around the classroom. I was being noisy. I was quarrelling with the person sitting next to me. I called out in class without putting my hand up first. I was rocking back and forth on my chair.«

Students who are not in possession of the necessary reading and writing skills at this stage are permitted to put a cross next to a series of pictograms. The next step requires the student to make suggestions for improving his learning and social behavior and to record these considerations in a plan laying out how he/she will return to class. Only by doing this will he/she be given permission to return to his/her class. When he/she does, he/she must present his/her completed plan to the teacher who has excluded him/her from the class. After considering what the student has written in his plan, the teacher will then decide whether the student is allowed to rejoin the lesson. If the student goes on to disrupt the class again, then the entire process is repeated.

If the student is sent to the training room three times in all, then his parents or guardians are summoned to the school for a training room meeting. This discussion will only take place during the training room's opening times. If a student refuses to enter the training room, he will be suspended from the school with immediate effect. He will only be allowed to return to the school once a training room meeting has taken place. If a student refuses to leave the school after he has been informed of his suspension, Balke (2003, pp. 41-42) recommends the police be called: they will then remove the student from the premises.

Numerous ministries and education authorities together with academics in their roles as political advisers (e.g., Klemm and Preuß-Lausitz, 2011, p. 105; Preuß-Lausitz 2011, p. 108) recommend the implementation of the TRP or comparable programs in inclusive schools in order to effectively implement the UN convention particularly in respect to students with emotional and social needs.

The purpose of this summative or outcome evaluation is to look at the results of the TRP, at the degree to which it accomplishes its specific goals, at the educational value and impact of the TRP, and what might point to changes that should be made in order to improve the program in subsequent implementations or when planning new programs and interventions. The objectives of this evaluation lie in the answers to the following questions: What is the impact on students with emotional and social needs? What is the overarching impact across the teaching and learning processes in a class? What is the impact on the teachers? What is the overarching impact across the broad culture of the school?

For methodological considerations, the author draws on the literature which evaluates education programs (Patton 2002; Wall 2014; Yarbrough et al., 2011). From these sources, the author has selected a »status design« to determine the current state of affairs regarding the TRP in German schools. The procedure used to collect data to answer the evaluation questions listed above included the following: A review and examination of all available material including the program descriptions and instructions which are currently in use, critical discussion papers by other authors (Goeppel 2002; Jornitz 2004; Pongratz 2010), radio broadcasts and television reports which have examined the program critically, and quantitative studies looking into the effectiveness of the TRP (Balz 2004; Wollenweber 2013).

Additionally, the author drew on qualitative data which he collected over several years at two schools which use the TRP by systematically observing the »training rooms« as well as the classes being taught at these schools, together with the participative observation of staff meetings. Furthermore, the author evaluated »focus groups« (Patton 2002, pp. 385-390) with teachers in the context of in-service training courses which the author ran at various schools and across the various school types. Primary importance here was given to the »decision-making model«. Additionally, the author made use of the »transactional model« (e.g., Patton 2002, pp. 171-172), by involving people who had been directly affected by the TRP and by exploring their different perspectives.

The TRP evaluation undertaken here has its theoretical basis in the disciplines of critical-constructivist education and teaching methodology, especially where Klafki (2007), in the German context, sourced and developed the philosophical ideas of the Enlightenment, the educational concepts of Classicism and the socio-critical currents of educational philosophy in the 20th century. Here, the educational ideal is aligned with the principle of responsible freedom in the Kantian sense.

Against this background, education signifies the ability of the students to act autonomously, to participate actively and to promote solidarity with others. In cases where children and adolescents come from unstable social environments, as is often the case with students with emotional and social needs, efforts to educate them must have an emancipatory character in order to increase their chances of social integration. A comparable approach has been developed in the United States under the heading »Teaching for Social Justice« (e.g., Michie 2004, 2009). It involves the creation of an enabling, empowering pedagogy which can address students' life situations, their cultural contexts, their social and economic upheavals, their life experiences and problems.

All this takes place on the basis of good educational relations and on the basis of a project-orientated and participative teaching methodology in the course of which students are actively involved in cooperative learning whilst participating in the design and development of the whole teaching and learning process. Klafki's work also includes these kinds of practical, educational approaches, as does the literature on inclusive education (e.g., Ainscow et al., 2006; Mastropieri and Scruggs, 2009).

A further theoretical point of reference in evaluating the TRP is provided by evidence-based knowledge in the field of education and teaching methodology for students with emotional, social and behavioral needs (e.g., Cole et al., 2013; Garner et al., 2014; Sailor et al., 2009;

Visser et al., 2012; Walker and Gresham, 2014). Any intervention which seeks to control a student's behavior must always be carefully considered to ensure that it is actually in keeping with the educational ideal described above. Foucault's (1995) critical discourse addressing the operational structures which are built into social institutions therefore represents an absolutely essential theoretical point of reference in this discussion paper (e.g., Pongratz, 2010).

What is the TRP's impact on students with emotional and social needs? Bründel and Simon do not specify what they understand by a good lesson. Balke (2003), in contrast, defines a good lesson in reference to Csikszentmihalyi (2008) as being one that »flows«, in which the students are completely and enthusiastically involved, and where they are immersed in the subject matter. Now, to safeguard the learning flow for the majority of the class, the one student who is obviously unable to find a point of access to this learning flow and so does something else, something unexpected and therefore disruptive, must leave the classroom. Having been separated from his/her class and sent to the training room, the student must think of reasons why he/she has been unable to find a way into the learning flow in which his/her classmates now find themselves.

But was it actually even possible for this supposedly disruptive student to find a point of access to the general learning flow of this class? Were the exercises and the material provided explained in a way that was appropriate for this student? Did the teacher really provide the necessary educational support? Was the educational relationship between the teacher and the student sufficient to make the student feel that the teacher was being encouraging and supportive? Did the teacher really invest the necessary care in adapting the material to the abilities of the student? Did the teacher make available active approaches to dealing with the material, as well as forms of cooperative learning and interaction with other students? Would it not have been more appropriate from the start to develop a learning flow which would have included all the students in the class? Did the teacher make every effort to identify what a learning flow might look like for this particular student?

In actual fact, the TRP seems to make the one student who is apparently not functioning in the class responsible for the failure of the lesson. It is this one student who must undergo a process of change and adapt to the prevailing conditions within which the teaching and learning process is taking place. The mechanisms of the TRP force the student to discipline himself (Jornitz 2004, p. 109). The world of the TRP simply does not take into account the complexity and interplay between the manifold conditions and factors existent in a teaching and learning context of this kind, where the conduct of the teacher is also of crucial importance. The following statement made by one of the teachers in the focus groups reflects this attitude: »Since we introduced the TRP I am very pleased to say that the students who used to be consistently disruptive in class have been forced to give up their disruptive behavior.«

If the student wishes to leave the training room again, he is forced into a state of »documented conformity« (Jornitz 2004, pp. 109-110). He is forced to acknowledge his disruptive behavior and then to put down his good intentions in writing in order to be granted permission to return to his class. Only by doing this can he escape the stigma of being the outsider. Even if the literature dealing with the TRP makes reference to a »negotiated return«, in reality the student has nothing to negotiate. Goeppel (2002, p. 52) sees the student's position as being downgraded to that of a »supplicant«. How honest and sustainable are the promises the student makes to improve his/her behavior when they are written down under duress in the training room?

Furthermore, the process of clarification takes place at one remove from the classroom, in an entirely different place. This approach will not provide any long-term solutions. Jornitz (p. 117) states that there will be a boomerang effect and the problem will come back again. This is because the teacher who excluded the student from the class in the first place should be involved in finding the solution.

A 14-year-old Roma boy with emotional and social difficulties was sent to the training room on dozens of occasions. The boy was aware of the fact that his parents had not previously attended a training room meeting and that they were unlikely to do so in the future. The reason given by the boy's parents was that they did not have access to a vehicle which they would need to travel to the rather remote, rural school. Towards the end of the series of training room exclusions, the boy was suspended from his school for a six-week period because the parents continued their refusal to attend a training room meeting at the school. When the school's inspector responsible heard of the situation, he found himself in a dilemma. On the one hand he had approved the introduction of the TRP at that school, but on the other hand the long period of suspension to which the boy was to be subjected as a result of the TRP was not in accordance with the statutory regulations at schools which were in force at the time. The committee which was normally required to meet to discuss long periods of suspension had not done so, neither had it debated the case, neither had this statutory committee taken an official decision. The positions between the family and the school became increasingly entrenched. When the situation became deadlocked, the school's inspector decreed that the boy move to a school in the adjacent school district. A school that acts in such a manner is exhibiting a disregard for the human right to education (Kenworthy and Whittaker, 2000). A »culture of silence« comes into being (Gibson 2006). Voices, like that of the Roma boy, fall silent.

The Training Room Program claims it encourages students to take responsibility for themselves and freely take their own decisions. Any student whose behavior continues to be at variance with the rest of the class even following a warning by the teacher has, as far as the TRP model sees the situation, decided of his own free will to leave the classroom and go to the training room. It was his own decision to go (Bründel and Simon, 2003, p. 44). But are boys or young men with extremely problematic family backgrounds, where abuse is taking place and where the youngsters are traumatized etc., truly able to behave with such a high degree of responsibility and freely take decisions for themselves?

Claßen and Nießen (2006, p. 92), as well as Bründel and Simon (2007, p. 144) also recommend using the TRP in contexts where children with attention problems and hyperactivity are present. Claßen and Nießen in particular argue that the straightforward structure of the TRP and the way in which it imposes order lowers the level of excitability among children suffering from ADHD. But can teachers really hold these children fully responsible for their behavior, considering the specific complexities of their conditions?

Claßen and Nießen (2006) are stigmatizing children and adolescents with emotional and social needs when they write on the back of their book: »Nobody should suffer from *antisocial* behavior.« In order to provide this group of young people with genuine opportunities for learning and personal development, this kind of deficit thinking must be dismantled (Garcia and Guerra, 2004). In this context, highly critical statements were voiced in the focus group containing teachers: »I don't get the impression that the students have very much respect for the idea of the TRP. But they know they have to adhere to its rules. Of course the TRP has meant that we have some quieter classroom sessions than we did in the past. But quite a bit of the communicative spontaneity and authenticity has been lost in our interactions with the students. Their relationship with us teachers is now more strategic and less open than it used to be. In the eyes of the students we have turned into technicians who are operating a machinery of power. Students who come from seriously problematic backgrounds simply do not understand what we are doing and why we are doing it.«

What is the TRP's impact across the teaching and learning processes in a class? Let us examine several statements voiced by teachers in one of the focus groups. One point of view that was aired on more than one occasion was the following: »Now that we have the TRP, the students have a clearer point of reference telling them what constitutes good classroom behavior«. But there was also a degree of concern, as we can see in the following statement which was made by another teacher: »The TRP directs the perceptions and thought processes of all students towards a model of conformity. The omnipresence of these rules and the constant feeling in the room that a disruptive classmate might be excluded from the class dominates the attentiveness of the students. If a child is rocking back and forth on their chair then other students immediately start looking demonstratively at the poster on the wall listing the rules, reminding me by doing so of my responsibility to finally begin the questioning ritual which will get the errant student back on track. My old ideas about teaching are of no use to me any more as a specialist teacher. I have the feeling as though the whole student body has become conditioned since we introduced the TRP.«

The TRP has an impact across the entire teaching and learning process in a class because all of the students in a school with the TRP have one specific educational experience. They learn that those students who are not sufficiently in a position to adapt to the prevailing conditions in the teaching and learning process must leave the class in order to then subject themselves, outside the classroom, to a process of self-discipline. The students also observe that there is no deeper, fundamental educational consideration given to the processes at work in the classroom and the students' social experiences underlying them. The learning behavior expected from the students within the parameters of the TRP can be characterized as follows: »I am quiet and pay attention. I sit at my desk. I look to the front of the class and follow the lesson. When I wish to say something, I raise my hand« (Bründel and Simon, 2007, p. 99).

In the referential world of the TRP, the concept of movement which is integral to many educational games and cooperative, interactive forms of learning, no longer seems to exist. Bründel and Simon (2003, p. 29) portray a situation in which the necessary processes of clarification and consideration which arise in a more pedagogically orientated classroom actually run contrary to their conception of teaching in the sense of academic instruction. The achievements of German educational theory since the 1970s have been displaced, including independent, process-orientated, cooperative student-orientated and real-world-orientated learning in which students could be active in discovering new knowledge for themselves. There is no place here for student participation, student voice and empowerment projects (Nind et al., 2012; Robinson and Taylor, 2012; Scanlon 2012; Sellman 2009), just as there is no space in classroom teaching to address the children's particular social and cultural backgrounds from which their specific social, emotional and behavioral difficulties emerge in the first place (Michie 2004, 2009). Instead, the concepts of uniformity, conformity and discipline prevalent in the 1950s are being revived once again.

What is the TRP's impact on the teachers? In summarizing the main result of his empirical study, a survey of teachers, Balz (2004, p. 2) states that teachers find the TRP helpful. Bründel and Simon (2007, p. 151) use the results of Balz's study to underscore the positive effects of the TRP: »Teacher satisfaction with the program: 89%, reduction in classroom disruption: 82%, improvement in the quality of lessons: 72%, improvement in the classroom atmosphere: 73%.« These results are of limited validity. Simply asking the teachers in schools with the TRP about the program after a relatively short time-span certainly does not provide a comprehensive and conclusive picture.

In his empirical study on the effectiveness of the TRP, Wollenweber (2013) found neither positive effects on the behavior of the children nor any significant improvement for teachers. There was no reduction in the numbers of sick days taken by teachers, something which Bründel and Simon used in their argumentation to indicate teachers' exposure to high levels of stress. But there is no solid empirical evidence for the effectiveness of the TRP with regard to improvements in the work-related and social behavior of the students in the classroom.

Statements made by teachers in the focus groups suggest that the TRP can result in a hardening of teachers' attitudes: «I like being able to get rid of very disruptive students simply and easily. Unfortunately, our school runs an internal policy stating that only one student from any given class can be sent to the training room at any one time. But if things get a bit out of hand in the fifth or sixth lesson I just wait until the one student has returned from the training room with his plan before sending the next one there. Lots of working hours have been invested in the training room that are no longer available for creating small, differentiated study groups, and the colleagues just sitting there in the training room can also do something for their money.« Another teacher said: »Relations with my students have become more superficial and distant since we introduced the TRP. I am starting to see the students as objects. They mean less to me emotionally than before. My attitudes have hardened. That's the only way I can serve the system. That is a loss.«

The TRP cannot result in long-term, durable improvements because it is based on a negative, deficient image of young people. Bründel and Simon (2003, p. 14) write that nowadays, in general, students lack expertise and a sense of responsibility and that young people have become used to blaming others for their own failures. The two authors use euphemistic phrases such as »the students do not know…«, »the students are unaware of…«, »the students have not learned to…«. The TRP channels the teachers' awareness in the direction of these deficits and the resulting breaches of school rules. In the end, the questioning ritual envisaged by the Training Room Program ends up governing the teacher's perceptions, thoughts and actions: »What are you doing? What does the rule state? How are you going to decide? If you disrupt the class again, what's going to happen then« (Bründel and Simon, 2007, p. 42)?

What is the TRP's impact across the broad culture of a school? Are the designers of the Training Room Program really interested in freedom? This seems highly questionable when reading the profoundly self-contradictory Eisenhower quotation which the authors use to elucidate the management principles which form the basis of the TRP: »Leadership is the art of getting someone else to do something you want done because he wants to do it« (Bründel and Simon, 2013, p. 15). Surprisingly, Bründel and Simon (2003, p. 134) claim that the Training Room Program is »thoroughly steeped in humanist thinking« even though freedom and humanism are very strongly related. Let us read a statement on this subject by a teacher in one of the focus groups: »I am pleased we adopted the TRP. Now we can take really decisive action. Now we've finally got rid of that damned freedom-orientated education. I always hated having to negotiate with the students. Now the focus has returned to the class subject and it was about time after the PISA-shock!«

It seems to be rather more the case that the conception of the human being in the TRP literature is that of someone who needs to be externally controlled and moulded into shape by the mechanisms within social institutions. It is the very same, pessimistic image of human beings being driven by their desires and instincts that we find in the works of Machiavelli and Hobbes, where only strong state institutions are in a position to control people of this kind and keep them in check. But are we entitled to limit freedom in the name of freedom? Pongratz (2010, p. 63) therefore sees the TRP as the practice of »governmental punishment«. For Jornitz (2004, p. 106), the TRP's attitude to the subject of freedom seems like the »overdoor to a re-education camp«.

Hence, when the TRP was introduced into the school where another of our focus-group teachers was working, his reactions to the changes in his school culture were correspondingly negative: »The change in the culture of my school was a really difficult time for me. A large group of teachers who up to that point had really been instrumental in the formation of the school's climate of learning thanks to their project-orientated, attachment pedagogy, were pensioned off. Then a new, younger generation arrived and immediately began installing the TRP. They managed to establish a majority and get the principal on board too. Many of the middle generation teachers who had always found it hard to engage pedagogically with challenging students seemed to get a new lease on life. They suddenly started striding down the corridors with an entirely new sense of self-confidence.«

The bureaucratisation and archiving of personal data which goes hand in hand with running this program must also be critically examined. The TRP produces a potpourri of referral forms, self-evaluation questionnaires, students' plans for returning to their classes, and minutes taken during the discussions documenting the allegedly disruptive behavior of the students and how they intend to improve it. All of these documents are archived and serve as the basis for whatever actions are taken subsequently (Balke 2003, p. 87; Bründel and Simon, 2003, pp. 109 and 189). If we take recourse to Foucault's (1995) critical discourse, the generation of knowledge about individuals in the context of social institutions, and the generation of power, are very closely interconnected here.

The TRP requires all teachers in a school to be involved in the program in equal measure and to collaborate in its implementation (Bründel and Simon, 2003, p. 193). The program does not envisage individual approaches by single teachers. Of course, any one teacher can decide not to send his students to the training room, but if the duty roster determines that it is that teacher's turn to supervise the training room, then he has to carry out this duty whether he wants to or not. In a school which the author studied at close quarters over a period of two years, one teacher refused to carry out the task of supervising the training room because the program did not correspond with his pedagogical values. This resulted in him being forcibly transferred to another school district.

At another specialized school which the author studied, again over two years, one teacher reported the following: »A seven-year-old boy was brought to me crying and shouting in the training room by his class teacher. He crawled under the desk and cowered there. It seemed to me to be neither possible nor sensible to talk to the student about him writing out a plan detailing how he wanted to return to the class. Instead, I asked the boy about his interests. I waited. The boy stopped sobbing, stuck his head out and looked at me inquisitively. Then he told me about his interest in airports and of matters aeronautical. I suggested he draw an airport on the board in chalk. As he was drawing, the seven-year-old commented on his picture and I was impressed by his enormous expertise on the subject. I asked him questions about what he was drawing, whereupon he went into even greater detail on the subject. When the class teacher collected the boy at the end of the lesson, I presented him to her without any written self-evaluation and with no plan for his return to the classroom. She reported this to the school principal who then issued me with an official warning for undermining the school rules.«

In cases where teachers refuse to implement the TRP, Claßen and Nießen (2006, p. 32) seek to return them to the general path adopted by their colleagues by removing their recourse to the disciplinary measures which were previously enshrined in the statutory regulations for such situations. In particular, it is no longer possible to convene a meeting of the class committee consisting of the allegedly problematic child, his parents, the elected representative of the parents in the class, the elected representative of the school, the teachers concerned and often the school principal as well. The aim of this committee is to discuss the alleged problematic behavior of the student and to explore potential solutions. This committee can order a student's temporary suspension from the school or decide upon other disciplinary measures as laid down in the statutory regulations. It is important to note here that the participation of the school's and the parents' elected representatives provides a safeguard against any arbitrary decision-making by the school staff.

In contrast, the TRP operates outside the statutory regulations. Many schools in Germany have stopped working with attachment pedagogy. At the same time, these schools are making no effort to apply the knowledge base which currently exists internationally in the field with regard to the promotion of children's emotional and social development at school and in the classroom. Instead, they are reverting back to the principle of confrontation. They are practicing a rigid, punitive and paramilitary form of education (Herz 2012). These schools also readily adopt the TRP into their program. The »friendliness« which Bründel and Simon (2003, p. 50) continue to recommend no longer has a part to play in this process. On the contrary, the direction that education is now taking is being dictated by Ferrainola's principle of intervention which was practiced at the Glen Mills Schools for adolescents and which was predicated on *breaking their will*.

The author (Broecher 2016) has evaluated extensive qualitative data from a similar school: »Here, everybody is free to do what I want« is printed on a card on the door to the principal's office. The (female) principal stated assertively: »Here, everybody is helped, if necessary against their will.« A teacher at the school reported the following: »I already told you about my colleague, Mrs. Brandl, who sent one of her students, Nico, to me in the training room where he was supposed to stand on a piece of pink blotting paper for 40 minutes. As the teacher on duty, I was supposed to supervise this. After Mrs. Brandl had gone, I asked the student to sit down. I talked to him about the reasons that lay behind his being here and how he came to be in Schwarzegg. We also talked about his life situation at home. In the end he said to me: ›Nobody has ever talked to me like this at this school. When I came here to this school, my parents and I thought that they'd be able to help me. But you don't get help here. For most people it just makes things worse.‹«

In the context of a school culture like this one, the TRP becomes an instrument of dehumanization. Blunders of this kind reveal that something fundamental is missing from the program, namely a positive conception of human beings, a code of ethics, a pedagogical philosophy into which it is clearly written that the young people who attend a school might expect to receive truly respectable and seriously well-intentioned educational support, and not this kind of chicanery. Because the TRP itself circumvents the values of freedom and veracity, it is itself highly susceptible to corruption.

Apparently, the inclusion of students with emotional and social difficulties is to be furthered by schools reverting back to the old methods of exclusion, albeit temporary. Following the closure of ever more specialist special-needs schools, a new location must be found, away from the classroom, where disruptive students can be sent and where they will be subjected to some kind of special treatment. This place is called the »training room«. An idea is being revived from the time of segregated special education (Mousley et al., 1993) which was thought to have become obsolete long ago. The »cycle of exclusion« (Razer et al., 2013) which encompasses teachers and students alike therefore continues to exist. Old patterns of thinking are sustained. Those students who are unable to achieve the degree of conformity expected in the classroom are required to leave in order to practice their conformity outside the classroom.

This interconnection between formal inclusion and interior exclusion (Hodkinson 2012) must be called into question. Bründel and Simon (2007, p. 9) are convinced that the TRP arrived on the scene in German schools just at the right moment: »… at a time when a paradigm shift was taking place in education and psychology, away from the illusion that a teacher had to endure everything and that a school was a place where everyone should feel at ease« (Bründel and Simon, 2007, p. 9). Nevertheless, questions remain as to whether the TRP is an appropriate mechanism for fostering responsible, self-regulated behavior, because autonomy, self-determination and co-determination by the students is simply omitted.

The conceptual world of the TRP sees the students as objects, not as subjects with their own experiences and viewpoints. Any school which installs the TRP runs the risk of becoming a »disabling school« (Jauhiainen and Kivirauma, 1997) in which the processes of dehumanization (Malacrida 2005) can easily gain the upper hand. Why has the TRP become so widespread in Germany in particular, and not in other European countries, or in the United States? The reason might lie in the two parallel historical strands which have driven German pedagogical thinking and actions in the past. By making reference to Merseburger's (2005) Weimar studies, we can trace these two developmental strands back to the polar opposites of »mind« and »power«. In the »mind« category we would find Anna Amalia, Johann Wolfgang von Goethe and Friedrich von Schiller. In contrast, the concentration camp situated on the Ettersberg in direct proximity to Weimar would represent the »power« category: the mechanised, organised, bureaucratised, insensate subjugation and elimination of any deviations from the norm.

Education as shaped by the humanities has ceased to exist wherever the TRP has been implemented in schools. Gone are the educational traditions which were rooted in Classicism and the Enlightenment on the one hand, and in the socio-critical discourse of Adorno, Horkheimer, Fromm and Marcuse through to Habermas and Honneth on the other. Instead of entering into a process of self-reflection with students in the classroom, the new school environment, under the inauspicious influence of the TRP, produces conformity and a »pathology of normality« (Fromm 2011). The »mechanics of power« (Foucault 2001), as constructed and implemented by the TRP, forces all those teachers who still abide by their deeper pedagogical beliefs which are based on the principle of freedom, into a position of protest (to the point of being forcibly transferred!) or silence. Control and subjugation, including that of the teachers themselves, have become the dominant principles.

Perceived disruptions in the educational practice of teaching and learning in school can also serve as the wellspring for deeper cognitive processes when teachers understand how to address and work through the events that take place in their classrooms, together with the social and cultural processes which underlie them. After all, all students have much to learn from this kind of approach to teaching and education and, guided by a spirit of cognitive curiosity in the classroom, there is good reason to believe that students' destructive behavior will decline and their constructive behavior will increase, together with the inclusive energy of the entire school community. In cases in which children's and adolescents' emotional and social development is particularly vulnerable, it is imperative to create a good, stable educational bond; to give careful consideration to engaging with their emotional and social needs; to arrange an appropriate learning environment and to develop an appropriate teaching methodology (Boorn et al., 2010; Broecher 2015 a; Cooper 2011; Doyle 2003; Popp et al., 2011).

All of these points can be supported by teachers' interventions to direct and stabilize student behavior which already exist in the form of School-wide Positive Behavior Support (Broecher 2015 b; Hill and Brown, 2013; Sailor et al., 2009), interprofessional work (e.g., O'Connor 2013), family participation (e.g., Lewis 2009; Sheldon and Epstein, 2002) and community work (e.g., Klein 2000). It is upon this basis that concepts need to be explored for the professional development of teachers who have been in the school system for a longer period and who now find themselves confronted with the inclusion of students with emotional and social difficulties (e.g., Lane et al., 2014; Naraian et al., 2012) so that they no longer see the need to reach for a time-out model of such questionable efficacy as the Training Room Program.

5 When Children Plan a Trip on Their Own

What ideas do children have and what do they imagine when allowed to plan a trip on their own? In the following case study, a father makes the gift of a one-week travel voucher to each of his two sons, with the proviso that the two boys must individually plan a summer vacation trip to take separately with the father. The father takes notes on the planning process that soon gets under way. The object under examination is a 360-page journal, made available by the family in question and kept jointly by the father with his two sons (13 years and 9 years old) for an entire calendar year, starting with the Christmas when the children received the travel voucher as presents. The journal records everything from detailed notes on the preliminary thinking to daily entries during both trips.

As both boys gradually develop ideas for their respective trips and discuss them with their father, they reread journals kept during past years and reflect on them. The father made the following entries: »Jack had stacked up the older journals of our previous father-son travels next to his bed and began to read in them. He called my attention to a drawing that I made in the harbor of Cagliari on Sardinia: ›I can still remember exactly when you did that‹, he says ... ›Look, dad, here is what I wrote down in South Tyrol when I was just 8 years old‹ (reading now): ›For breakfast I had a pot of hot chocolate and dad ordered English tea. It was a little comfort in view of the thick rainclouds outside our window. Hiking was still out of the question... so we sat in the inn's public room and played checkers‹ (February 21).«

These older journals also cover travels undertaken by this West German family as a unit and include impressions recorded on those occasions by the mother, e.g., during a trip to France three years earlier. The mother made these entries: »I had looked forward to it for a long time. I was really excited when we saw the city limit sign for Giverny. Then we entered the village where Claude Monet bought a house and set out a garden. This is also where he painted his famous pictures of water lilies. Just the place by itself is beautiful. Hollyhocks line all the streets, in white, pink, and dark red... Then finally came the big moment: The pink stucco house with the green shutters and doors, the garden terrace... flowers everywhere, in the most gorgeous colors. Roses and hollyhocks in chaotic profusion on the flower beds. We were in luck, for the sun was shining and made the colors glow... .«

These insights from the older journals, retroactively worked into the text made available by the family, furnish information about the familial and cultural backdrop against which the boys developed the two trips described in this article. To begin with, it was necessary to distill out of the whole set of materials that which had relevance for the planning and execution of the two father-son journeys facilitated by the voucher gifts. To this end, the material was examined using qualitative content analytical methods to filter »themes« from the journal text (Patton 2002).

First, the text of 88,500 words was divided into smaller units. Next, the intertwined narrative threads, i.e., the alternating retrospectives, descriptions of the present, and plans for the future, were disentangled, examined one by one, and then reintegrated. This step also involved labeling themes and assigning the material to overarching thematic categories identified, namely: retrospectives of earlier travels by the father with his first-born son, retrospectives of earlier travels by the whole family, descriptions of the family's current day to day life, current processes of planning and reflecting as they relate to the two father-son trips in the planning stage, as well as subsequent documentation and retrospectives for these two trips planned by the children that are in focus here.

The next step consisted of finding »patterns« (Patton 2002) within these two thematic areas constituted by the newly-planned father-son trips with the travel vouchers as their starting points. While the father's and older son's Ireland trip is documented exclusively with summarizing notes, i.e. daily reports, the journal contains close to 150 pages of transcribed tape recordings of the Berlin trip with the younger son. These transcripts contain alternating summary reports, but mostly scenic impressions from the Berlin explorations and dialogues between father and son. The father made the following entry in this connection: »We had the idea to pack a voice recorder so we could record our impressions and observations, questions and thoughts on tape as we roamed through Berlin... to give us authentic notes that would reflect something of actual experience in the specific situation (August 8).«

Therefore, for the Ireland trip, a more synoptic type of text was created that is hence less voluminous, while exceptionally comprehensive, richly detailed documentations exist for the Berlin explorations. In structuring and categorizing the material bearing on both trips in focus here, particular attention was paid to the approach that each boy now took in planning and implementing his trip.

Now let us look at how thirteen year old Jack planned his trip. Already that December, the boy formulated first tentative thoughts for an in-depth exploration of the British Isles. As we learn from the journal, this interest was awakened by a Scotland trip that Jack had made as an eight year old together with his father. As January went by, Ireland crystallized as the travel destination. Jack envisioned being in the fresh air all day long and hiking by the Atlantic. In February, they booked flights to Kerry. In April, they bought a guidebook to the Kerry Way and became familiar with the individual stages of their trek. They booked first-night accommodations in June. All the rest was left to serendipity.

In late July, father and son flew to Kerry and hiked from Killarney to Waterville, by way of Kenmare, Sneem and Caherdaniel. Every day, they backpacked all their gear and turned in at guest houses in the evenings (Fig. 5.1). They passed the day in Sneem on account of steady rainfall, spending the time reading, having tea, and journaling.

Upon arrival in Waterville, their end stage destination, they spent one last day by the sea. They enjoyed the breathtaking scenery of the summery Atlantic and its very gentle August surf. They waded in the water, perched on rocks or took in the ever-changing pastel colors of the evening sky, father and son, each in himself, following his own thoughts, now and then conversing, as for example over dinner in the pub. The journal describes it all in detail:

»We slowly made our way up into the mountains. For a while, it was a karstic, rough landscape... then came blooming, lush meadows again with a rich diversity of grasses and flowers. Small creeks bubbled from the hills. Often the old Kenmare Road would lead through marshy terrain... we encountered not a living soul from this point on... small rivers blocked our way that we had ... to leap across on boulders... (August 1). After leaving Kenmare, crossing an old stone bridge we headed up into the hills again. The way led through brush, past hedgerows, thistles, and ferns. Often, we had to go over fences and stone walls with the help of step ladders put there for the purpose... across pastures, past grazing cattle we went, all the time heading up the mountain. But once we arrived on the summit, we were rewarded by the incomparable view of the Kenmare River, an elongated sea lough. Under the bright summer sky, the soft green hills stretched all around us; those farther in the distance were a bluish grey. The fresh breeze blowing here dried the sweaty brow... Mr. Teahan welcomed us in the friendliest of ways to the Derry East farmhouse. We took a twin room in the attic and were then invited to tea and crumpets in the lounge. We chatted briefly... signed up for the evening's dinner... (August 2). Late in the afternoon we stood in a narrow street with tightly packed houses... a quaint pub, a small grocery store... fortunately, a guesthouse... this time Jack asked for the room... in the pub, it was rustic and relaxed... some Irish families tarried by the bar, a passel of children revolving around them, licking green water ices (August 4).«

Now we turn to how nine-year old Peter approached his trip planning. In late December the boy started to develop ideas for his one week trip that were inspired by lesson content from his elementary school general studies class: »›Take a look in your room, Dad‹, Peter called out to me from upstairs, just as I walked in the front door... on my desk lay a folded-up letter... ›Dear Dad, when we were studying North Rhine-Westphalia in school, I thought about visiting monuments. I don't know if we can get there by train; if not, we can always take our car. Where do I want to go? Hint: Check the Travel Box in your room! Peter.‹ I went over to the file and in it I found his elementary school general studies textbook... with a bookmark sticking out of it. I picked up the book and opened it to the marked page. There, in large block letters was written ›E 4‹... just then, Peter entered my room, came over to me and flipped to the next page in the book to show me a photo of the ›Egge Rocks‹. Peter: ›Could be really interesting.‹ He pointed to a map just below the picture. ›Here, these are the hiking trails in red. And there is also a youth hostel. We could stay there and in the morning hike up that red trail to the Egge Rocks. And here are some burial mounds...‹, all the while his finger moved across the map grids (December 27).«

With undiminished enthusiasm, the nine year old continues planning, even if ultimately the focus on this first travel destination would dissolve into a Berlin trip. On multiple occasions in the ensuing weeks, father and son would talk about Berlin, about historical and political problems that had to do with the former zones that divided the city after the Second World War, the »Airlift«, the GDR or the »Wall«. They pull books off the shelves, look things up and talk about them. Sometimes it is Peter and at other times his father driving the talks and the research. They listen to Marlene Dietrich sing »I still keep a suitcase in Berlin« and conclude that it is full of longing. They phone a Russian lady from whom they rent a pied à terre on Brüderstraße for a week (Fig. 5.2). Peter studies the city map to find out how best to get from the Zoo train station to Brüderstraße.

During the actual Berlin exploration then accumulates a dense staccato of tape-recorded observations, thoughts and questions, an ongoing dialogue between father and son. The following scene reflects this in exemplary fashion. It is late evening. Father and son have just returned to their flat from the Museum at Checkpoint Charlie: »We helped ourselves to something to drink from the refrigerator and sank into the armchairs in the living room. Father: ›All the things that people used in escaping from the GDR!‹ Peter: ›I would never have done that.‹ Father: ›Why not?‹ Peter: ›It would have been too dangerous for me.‹ Father: ›And you would have stayed in the GDR?‹ Peter: ›Not really all that much either.‹ Father: ›Could you get used to the restrictions on people there? I know you are also someone who loves his freedom very much.‹ Peter: ›It's hard to say.‹ Father: ›Unbelievable, all the things they came up with: homemade airplanes…‹ Peter: ›…a hot air balloon sown together out of many cloth strips. That must have been a lot of work.‹ Father: ›The two families that drifted across the border in the homemade balloon. I have a lot of respect for that much courage!‹ Peter: ›And the balloon even caught fire on one side.‹ Father: ›But the boy put out the fire with a fire extinguisher. A real hero!‹ Peter: ›And they just made it‹ (August 18).«

Father and son are constantly on the go through the city, snap pictures, make sketches and take notes. Peter can't get enough of the program. He is curious about everything and enjoys the kaleidoscopic activities, although he also very much likes kicking back in the apartment (Fig. 5.5). The spectrum of their explorations covers roughly the following: The Natural History Museum with its dinosaur skeletons and mineral collections; the Museum of Technology with its »Rosinenbomber« (Raisin Bomber) (Fig. 5.8), steam locomotives (Fig. 5.10), Imperial Train, antique train tickets and historical windmills (Fig. 5.6), TV sets, and radios (Fig. 5.9); the Wall Museum with multimedia of the risky escape attempts from the GDR (Fig. 5.11 and 5.12); the Jewish Museum, Pergamon Museum, Old National Gallery, and Düppel, the medieval museum village. Other objects they explore include the boarded-up GDR Palace of the Republic (it was the year 2003) (Fig. 5.3), the Imperial Palace Square, the Brandenburg Gate, and the Reichstag building.

In late evening, father and son lie on the latter's roof under the glass cupola, looking up into the starry skies and ruminating about politics (Fig. 5.4). They tour the Potsdam palaces and reconstruct Voltaire's sojourn at Sanssouci. While walking down the street named Unter den Linden, the father explains the classical building style to the son. Sipping cool drinks, they sit in their prefab building apartment late into the night, with the windows open to the warm summer breeze, debating if it would be better to reconstruct the Imperial Palace in its original form or to restore the Palace of the Republic instead.

Stimulated by their visit to the Märkisches Museum, they try to imagine what the Brüderstraße, where they are staying, would have looked like 100 or 200 years ago, with its milliner's shops, small workshops, and horse-drawn wagons, and what the contemporary mindset would have been in the neighboring Nicolaihaus. Mornings, they sleep in a bit late and eat a leisurely breakfast, but soon they are filling a back-pack for the day, and then they dive once more into the cultural and historical universe that is Berlin. On two evenings, Peter and his father go swimming at the legendary Wannsee beach, humming the lyrics from the song »Pack' die Badehose ein...« (Pack your swimming trunks...).

The Third Reich is a key subject complex that Peter and his father repeatedly grapple with during the week. The journal documents the following dialogue from the Museum of Technology: »Peter: ›Can we listen to number 11 now?‹ Father: ›That is about the burning of the books.‹ Peter: ›Why did they do that?‹ Father: ›The Nazis fought against freedom of the mind and wanted to stifle any kind of criticism. That is why they burned books.‹ (A voice shouting ... ›I give into the fire the writings of Heinrich Mann ... Erich Kästner...‹) Peter: ›They burned Erich Kästner's books, too? What was so bad about ›Emil and the Detectives‹?‹ Father: ›Not a thing. But Kästner also published some other, critical texts. That was the problem‹ (August 16).«

Another exchange regarding the Third Reich that takes place in the Jewish Museum: »Father: ›The Freudenheim family of Berlin emigrated in 1938... And Fritz, 12 years old, recorded it. He drew a world map, in color even, and he drew in the route by which they traveled... via Hamburg... Lisbon... Casablanca...‹ Peter: ›The first thing he drew was a locomotive.‹ Father: ›That's right, they went by train.‹ Peter: ›From Berlin.‹ Father: ›...Then they crossed the ocean to Brazil... and finally to Montevideo, in Uruguay... That is how the boy dealt with his eventful childhood, by writing down everything...‹ Peter: ›There, in front, he also signed his picture. See that? Fritz Freudenheim‹ (August 19).«

A special highpoint for Peter during their Berlin explorations is the post windmill (Fig. 5.6) on the open air grounds of the Museum of Technology. Father and son engage in an intensive conversation with the museum docent in charge of the mill, delving into the historical background and functioning of this mill type. Using a sophisticated mechanism, the mill can be turned to face into the wind. The journal reveals the following scene:»Mill docent: ›No, they couldn't afford a horse for turning the mill. Peter can actually do it... Peter... will turn the 30 tons.‹ Peter: ›The mill weighs 30 tons?‹ Mill docent: ›Yes... (He turns to Peter). Ok, man of action, are you ready?‹ We climb down the steep wooden stairs. The museum man gets a few things ready outside... pulls the sledlike wooden frame away from the boom. To keep it from skidding, the frame is held in place by a post, one of many driven into the ground in a circle around the mill. Next, he hooks up an iron chain between the boom and a rotatable wooden post that sticks up vertically in the frame. Lastly, the docent horizontally inserts a kind of lever, a two-by-four that is about 2.5 meters long and rounded on one end to allow a better grip, into the vertical post. Peter walks in a circle, pushes, the chain rattles, tightens, and winds around the vertical post and soon there is an intense, loud creaking above the mill's king post. The giant mill turns (Fig. 5.7)... Father: ›Did you have to use a lot of force?‹ Peter: ›No, not much. But you have to weigh something; otherwise the wood knocks you back‹ (August 17).«

Let us now consider the question if such trips impact family relationships. The research (Agate et al., 2009; Durko and Petrick, 2013; Shaw et al., 2008; West and Merriam, 2009; Zabriskie and Cormick, 2003) attributes positive effects on family relationships to shared recreational activities in general and shared travel experiences in particular.

It emerges from this family's journal that the father-son trips contributed substantially to improving the family climate, by helping to defuse occasional rivalries and conflicts arising between the two brothers. The journal contains a few passages that allude to the two boys' rivalries and quarrels. The father noted something to this effect: »At supper, I put on some Irish folk music in reference to the Ireland trip. Jack did not have much of a reaction to it. I believe he was not in a good mood because he had quarreled with his brother shortly before. Well, they'll put some distance between them soon enough (July 22).«

And harking back to earlier hiking trips in Italy's Cinque Terre area, the father made this entry: »Fishing boats bobbing... colorful, closely packed houses... Jack and Peter were always scooting ahead, with their telescoping poles ... They were so busy exploring the centuries-old stone path's twists and turns through the Cinque Terre hills that they had no time to fight. Still, these trips by the whole family are coming to an end. The boys' diverging interests barely are still reconcilable with one another (August 14).« The concept that both parents are acting on in concert is to separate the two boys for a week, with each child getting the father's or mother's undivided attention. The father made this entry: »The boy who is on a trip enjoys the father's exclusive devotion and the one staying at home has the mother's full attention (January 12).«

In addition, when it is the father only who takes off into the world with the sons, it helps relieve stress on the mother. The journal contains the following passage penned by the father on this topic: »The stress on my wife Laura from her many responsibilities at work, in the home, and raising children is currently very high. She is in favor of my pedagogic travel philosophy, namely by shifting parts of child raising into the world outside. She is absolutely convinced of the value of these undertakings and looks forward to catching her breath during our absence (January 20).« Even 9 year old Peter sees it as a chance for the mother's to catch her breath when one of the boys is on the road with the father: »Then mom has a whole week to relax and recover (February 22).«

When the father-son duos return home, there are many adventures to relate and experiences to share with the other family members. This gives all family members a chance to encounter each other in a new way and to learn from one another. Here is what the father wrote about it: »During supper, Jack told about their adventuresome hikes on the Kerry Way and how we sank up to our calves in mud or how we were pursued by peculiar insect swarms, with Peter listening to him spellbound... and Peter told about evening swims at the Wannsee bathing beach, with Jack prompting him for details. One brother pays renewed attention to the other and listens intently to him, while Mama smiles, enjoys the stories, and is glad to have her boys home again (September 2).«

There is much to suggest that traveling in a parent-child dyad fosters familial cohesion, especially when the parents succeed in embedding the individual experiences in an overall family narrative that integrates everyone. The father gives a pertinent example for this, when nine year old Peter asks him which travel experiences he, the father, views as especially positive ones? »Peter: ›So, what do you like to remember most?‹ Father: ›The youth hostel in Clichy. I recall the sweltering heat... how the beds sagged... and all of us in one room, and four nights at that! Exploring Paris, in mid-summer! It was so hot that even a sheet was too much as cover. Remember, I took my mattress off the metal frame and put it by the wide-open window. And all of us together on it finished reading Preußler's Krabat. Wasn't that great? And Mama always looked forward so much to her ›café au lait in the morning‹ (July 21).«

The travel experiences generated by the separate father-son dyads are thus stretched by the father into a larger whole by bringing in background experiences that all of them took part in, such as their explorations of the city of Paris. This is where the journal reveals that father-son travel can complement travels undertaken by the entire family. Traveling in individual father-son dyads thus serves to sustain familial cohesion and helps the parents achieve their pedagogical objectives, i.e., to foster each of their children's optimal development.

The research also suggests that travel has additional positive effects on children's intellectual or academic learning (e.g., Byrnes 2001; Newman 1996). This can happen through active exploration by children, of museums especially (e.g., Chang 2006, 2012; Gutwill and Allen, 2012; Haden 2010; Piscitelli 2001). These processes also have interactive dimensions involving the parents into which flow parental thinking and knowledge (Thomas and Anderson, 2013). Such positive effects are particularly underlined by the Berlin explorations of nine year old Peter. These explorations lead to the boy starting to develop pertinent questions, which is already an important step toward deeper academic learning.

The father made the following entry: »Peter looked at the roofs of the Potsdam palace and suddenly asked about the chemical processes that gave the roofs their light green color. ›Why are some parts of the roof light green instead of ranging from dark to black? Is it because the metal is different or some other oxidation process is happening?‹ he asked... On the ride back from Potsdam, Peter threw out questions about possibilities for speeding up light rail trains, about the difference in the engines or motors of light rail trains, subways and regular trains. He observed that subways are best at accelerating rapidly. But what special motors do they use here and what are the technical elements required?‹ (August 18).«

As evidenced by the following journal passage penned by the father some seven weeks later, Peter's Berlin explorations achieved a certain long-term sustained effect in terms of academic learning: »Peter comes into my room and tells me that he has looked some more into the acceleration technology used on subway trains. He had read something about it in a book... (October 6).«

Simultaneously, we are dealing here with an interaction between this type of educational travel on the one hand and academic learning at school on the other. In the initial phase of developing ideas for his trip, Peter did after all – via the previously mentioned »Egge Rocks« he learned about in class – once again draw on stimuli from his school lessons, even if he ultimately did not pursue the idea further: »At breakfast, Peter asked me about the Wartburg. Did I suppose that the inkblot left by Martin Luther was still there? What made him ask? It was because of his religion class. Mr. M., the religion teacher, told the story of how Luther hid from his pursuers in the Wartburg (Fig. 6.42) and how he translated the New Testament there. This inkblot happened during all that writing. It could still be seen today. He would like to explore it on the spot and maybe take a trip there (March 3).« These initial trip planning exercises of Peter's documented in the journal show the very important role that the work of primary school teachers plays in equipping children with models for exploring the world.

Now we will take into account the diversity of children's emotional, cognitive, and physical needs and developmental issues. The trip planned by the younger son is a kind of intellectual high altitude flight, a rapid fire intellectual ping pong between father and son, in which the father also functions as a role model for active explorative thinking and behavior. Take for example the following exchange between them on Berlin's Palace Square: »Father: ›There, the Palace of the Republic, you see over there, with the copper red reflective glass?‹ (Fig. 5.3) Peter: ›But they nailed the building shut with boards.‹ Father: ›That's right, the building has been empty for a while... I was inside it back in GDR times, sometime around 1981, having coffee. There, larger than life, is the GDR emblem: hammer, sickle, wheat garland, but the hammer and sickle are gone.‹ Peter: ›But I saw those symbols in a book‹ (August 15).« The subject of the former GDR occupies father and son at every turn. This was their dialogue at a flea market for books in front of Humboldt University: »Peter: ›FDJ? What was that?‹ Father: ›Free German Youth.‹ Peter: ›Free? In a prison?‹ Father: ›The FDJ was the big youth organization in the GDR. If you wanted to get ahead in that country, you had to belong.‹ Peter: ›Wow‹ (August 17).«

Peter and his father are walking toward the Brandenburg Gate: »Peter: ›See the angels up there?‹ Father: ›They're beautiful, silhouetted against the blue night sky... Now take a look at this facade. This, by the way, is what's called the classical style of architecture.‹ Peter: ›What is classical?‹ Father: ›This architectural style borrows elements from Greek and Roman antiquity. Those columns there, for instance. Do you know when antiquity was?‹ Peter: ›Yes. The time of Jesus, both just before and after... How old is the ›quadriga‹ up there on the Brandenburg Gate? Who actually made it?‹ (August 15).«

The following episode dates from their time spent at Berlin's Natural History Museum: »Peter: ›Here are measuring instruments!‹ Father: ›And what are they used for?‹ Peter: ›For measuring angles on crystals. There's so much to discover here!‹ Father: ›It must be heaven for students studying mineralogy. It's a magic world of colors.‹ Peter (eyes riveted on the artifacts): ›They can come anytime and look at everything‹ (August 15).«

Even with all the fascination that Peter's and his father's highflying intellectual exploration of Berlin holds, a child's needs can also overlap with areas of child development not involving intellectual learning, as the example of the Ireland trip makes clear. To sum up, comparatively speaking, two completely different stories or dimensions resulted from these two trips.

For 13 year old Jack, the daylong, challenging, and contemplative backpacking trek through southwest Ireland seems to be exactly the right kind of trip at the right time. It seems he had made a well thought-out plan with good awareness of his personal needs. The father reflected on this in a journal entry: »At no point did I have to do cheer Jack up with anything to boost his morale. No matter if we were outdoors hiking through the countryside or in our quarters for the night, Jack remained self-contained and in his inner world. I never heard from him: But this is boring. I want to do this or that now. Or: couldn't we just ...? He never said: How much farther is it? Or: I don't feel like going any farther. Jack was and is a very undemanding, relaxed, entirely wonderful travel companion. He seems to take things in stride and adapt to them (August 11).«

For Jack, his trek through western Ireland's remote coastal regions is more about putting some distance between himself and the school hubbub, about being immersed in peaceful nature (Fig. 5.1). This is precisely what the father had anticipated when he noted the following a few months prior to the Ireland trip: »...and when I see Jack sit at his desk poring over math or Latin homework, I am certain that during our joint trip he will prize engaging in as much physical activity as possible in the great outdoors« (April 4). Jack's Ireland trip is about meditating by hiking, about going into silence in which to find his self. Perhaps, other developmental issues are progressing or coming into balance during the daily contemplative hikes, processes that are not subject to being verbalized – or having to be.

Recalling Hannah Arendt (1998), the nature of the Irish walks could be designated as »vita contemplativa«; that of the Berlin excursions as »vita activa«, considering how much was taken on, conquered and set in motion, a post mill weighing tons included. On the one hand, this contrast could stem from the children's differing personalities. On the other, we also assume that a 13 year old boy goes through different developmental stages than a 9 year old goes through. Previous diary entries tell us that Jack, when he was just 9 years old, roamed fascinated for an entire day through the science and technology collections in Munich's Deutsches Museum on returning from a hike with his father in South Tyrol: »Often, it was possible to do an experiment by pushing a button or lever; for example, backing up the water in a simulated river behind a small dam, opening sluice gates, or pumping water up through transparent pipes. Many experiments dealt with weights, a body's center of mass, or the lever principle. Jack was full of enthusiasm and constantly communicated his ideas, questions, and thoughts about the physical phenomena.« From all this, it can be surmised that what matters most in planning such trips is remaining sensitive to the age-appropriate developmental themes and needs of the individual child, while simultaneously reacting constructively to potential personality differences.

Very few studies to date have examined an active role by children in planning and taking trips (e.g., Hilbrecht et al., 2008; Nickerson and Jurowski, 2001). The father in our case study, too, mostly handled the planning for earlier trips with Jack or travels with the entire family on his own. But, in this instance, linked with the idea of the two gift vouchers was the father's resolve to stay out of it this time. In the journal he wrote: »In addition, I'm going to approach the situation somewhat differently than to date… This time, the boys should take over as much of the trip planning and required preparations as feasible or even completely. The trip will largely be constituted the way each of the two boys plans and pictures it in his mind (December 21).«

The child's planning process moves ahead in small increments and takes time. Peter experimentally steps through potential scenarios and changes his mind again. The father entered the following in the journal: »Peter said, he wasn't sure if we would actually travel to the area that he had designated. For now, the plan remains in place (January 1).« While some elements of the plan still change multiple times, others remain constant throughout. From the start, Peter remained firm on the transportation method *train* and never questioned it during the entire planning window. The father already noted at Christmas time: »Peter, after having read the voucher text, affirmed: ›By train. I would like to go by train.‹ (December 26).« It often happens that when Peter and his father talk about their joint trip that the boy fetches a book or other atlas, to get a better notion of what was said earlier: »Immediately, Peter brings an atlas over to study the geography of Iceland… We sit in front of three open atlases that the boy had carted over, and we look at the Scandinavian countries (May 21).«

Whichever direction a child takes in his personal planning, if accompanied by a loving parent's appropriate support, it turns into an exercise in self-efficacy, decision making ability and action competence. At the same time, the children's autonomy operates within a bounded framework that responsible parents must also set and that will also be accepted, as the two children demonstrated here. On that subject, the father noted: »Naturally, I won't put up with all sorts of conceivable discomforts. I'm not twenty-five any more. I will certainly look after myself and speak up for my personal needs (December 21).«

Both sons test the limits of how far-flung a trip their father will permit. On that subject, we read in the journal: »Jack: ›Does Africa qualify?‹ Father: ›With just one week, I don't want to make a long distance flight. At most, that would mean North Africa‹ (December 31). Peter: ›Could we also go to the North Pole?‹ Father: ›That could be rather difficult. Let's just stick with Europe. So, the limit would perhaps be Iceland or Norway‹ (May 21).« The boys not only accept such boundary setting; it actually turns out to be stimulative, as the following passage from the journal documents: »Peter immediately fetches an atlas and studies Iceland's geography. He moves his index finger over the map. Peter: ›Here is the highest mountain.‹ Father: ›It's probably a volcano. Remember ›Voyage to the Center of the Earth‹, by Jules Verne?‹ Peter: ›Oh, yeah! Now that would interest me!‹ (May 21).«

Even with all of the individual initiative, autonomy and the children's participation in the travel arrangements, the parents always retain a certain, indispensable residual pedagogical responsibility. It can range from hiking boots to what goes in the backpack; after all, Jack and his father will be carrying all their baggage on their backs for a week. We take another look at the journal: »The new hiking boots are ready, but Jack has not tried them on once. I went to his room right away and suggested he wear the boots for a few hours, or better yet, wear them to school the next day, so break them early (May 18)... The departure time for the flight to Ireland approaches. Today, we spent two hours packing both backpacks. This has to be done very carefully and in a well-thought out manner, because we will be carrying everything that we'll need during the week on our backs (July 27).«

Of course, the subject of father-son travel has a great deal to do with emotional devotion to the child (John O'Donohue 1997, 1998), over and above all rational and practical planning. A child given the chance to plan a trip independently and then take it with the parent already experiences the parent's undivided attention for his or her person, thoughts, learning interests and needs in the planning stage but even more so when embarked on it.

Research accepts as non-controversial that children's development will be served when fathers actively and constructively engage with the upbringing and education processes of the family (e.g., Ball 2010; Downer et al., 2008; Gottzén 2011; Louv 1993; Milkie et al., 2010; Pattnaik and Sriram, 2010; Sriram 2011). Treating father-son trips as a recommended model in discussions in the field of parent education hence could encourage still more fathers to become actively involved in the family.

We can also assume that there will be positive repercussions for the father who engages in this way. He feels needed in his role as father and hence affirmed. From his engagement as father, he can realize meaning and perspective for himself during the father-son travel (e.g., Eggeben and Knoester, 2001; Harrington 2006). It also gives the father a chance to revert in a small way to being a boy again, to recall the little and great adventures of his own childhood and then in turn share this experience with his son in a real setting. In this respect, the father wrote in the journal kept four years earlier in Meran, South Tyrol: »In the tent, holding a flashlight, we read a Ludwig Thoma story about boy pranksters.«

In Ireland, Jack's quiet nature, moreover, has a healing effect on the father who is still stressed from his teaching duties. With the school year only just behind him, the teacher-father still tends to become too edgy intellectually and to start lecturing – by making an exercise for them both out of learning the English vocabulary from the Irish short stories he reads in the evening; or, after already having crafted his own poem on the day's impressions, trying to push the son also to write poetry. But there the boy, in his meditative-abstaining way, guides him gently back to what matters: The *road* that they are both on, the *silence*, and the *natural beauty* of the landscape, all things for which the child does not need a lot of words. And yet, as we discover from an older Sardinia journal, Jack, on a trip when he was all of nine years old, on his own initiative had in fact written a swash-buckling pirate story, inspired by the fort, the harbor and a mysterious tower in Cagliari where legend had it that pirates actually hid their ill-gotten gold. But now, on their hike through Ireland, this thirteen year old embodies the way of the *Tao* that means immersing yourself in the moment. Jack becomes co-therapist with an Irish landscape to help ground the father again and renew his contact with himself and his own inner world in the course of a week of back-packing.

Parents who wish to plan such an enterprise with one of their children, be it a father going on a trip with his son or his daughter, or be it a mother with her daughter or her son, may find they are not able to free up an entire week for just the one child. Let us hope that still leaves the option of at least a weekend to be planned and spent in the manner described here! In addition, there might also be economic constraints on a family. But children will automatically plan in line with what is possible to turn the project into reality. The father in our case study also puts economic considerations in play. Jack immediately accepts the constraints and even interprets them positively, as the following journal passage demonstrates: »Father: ›Rental cars are expensive, and they have the drawback that we'll have fewer chances to start conversations with local people than if we move by train or bus, not to speak of doing lots of walking. Not having a rental car, of course, can also be more uncomfortable at times.‹ Jack: ›There's nothing wrong with a little adventure‹ (February 20).«

All that matters to the child is the caring attention: having his or her mental world taken seriously, a personal interest shown, engaging in conversation, and being made time for. There is no need for a luxurious hotel or an expensive flight. All that it basically takes are sturdy shoes and a backpack. Whatever is embarked on then – a city ramble, a nature walk, a tent put up outdoors, shared contemplation of a sky full of stars – the child will be motivated as long as father or mother are the benign and interested companions at least until adolescence sets in and other issues impinge. What matters at this stage, nine year old Peter expresses just as the journal ends: »Father: ›What advice would you give other children, based on your personal travel experiences?‹ Peter: ›Be alert and curious, observe closely, and ask questions...‹ Father: ›What should adults do to help kids in these explorations?‹ Peter: ›Just be there for the child‹ (October 21).«

Figure 5.1

»In Killarney where it starts, the Kerry Way in southwest Ireland is still a walk in a well-cared for park, but then the landscape turns wilder around Sneem, Caherdaniel, and Waterville. In some parts, you navigate bogs, scree and watercourses, in others you sink in mud and struggle through brush and across livestock pastures. Stopping in a small town in the evening, taking a room and stopping for a bite in a pub compensates for all the exertions, but nothing can beat having a happy, satisfied boy next to you at table digging with gusto into his supper« (the father's notes).

110 | Creating Learning Spaces

Figures 5.2 and 5.3

»That we would rent an apartment in the history-steeped Brüder Street as base for our Berlin exploration was pure happenstance. It turned out to be a prefab concrete apartment building directly adjoining the Nicolai House. This meant we had the historic transitions from Wilhelmine Prussia all the way to the GDR that was situated around us close enough to touch. Prints and city models in Berlin's museums helped us reconstruct how life was lived in Brüder Street« (Fig. 5.2)…

»In that summer of 2003, when I set out to explore Berlin with my younger son, the former GDR's cultural centerpiece, the Palace of the Republic still occupied the place where Berlin's ›Stadtschloss‹ (the Imperial Palace) had formerly stood. When we found ourselves in this very spot, I told the boy about my train trip to West Berlin in 1981 with the diploma I had just received in my pocket. One day I rode over into East Berlin, changed a prescribed amount of money into German East Marks and used some of it to pay for a coffee in the Palace of the Republic bar. With the rest of the money I bought a biography of Rosa Luxemburg in a bookstore on Alexanderplatz« (the father's notes) (Fig. 5.3).

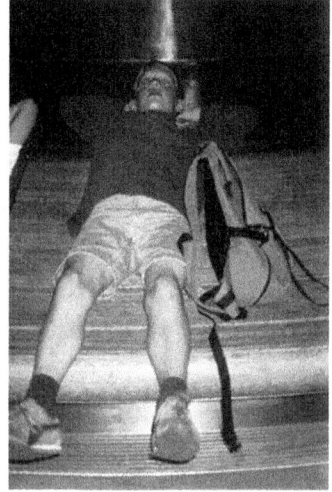

Figures 5.4 and 5.5

»Christo's wrapping of the historically significant Reichstag had already made the building the focus of familial conversations. Now to lie down ourselves under its glass dome and gaze up into the starry skies over Berlin made the experience much more intensive. But also the view down into the parliamentary room, made possible by the transparent glass architectonic design, brought in its train a long talk in our Brüder Street apartment about the importance of fair, transparent and down-to-earth politics« (Fig. 5.4)…

»Back in Brüder Street after a long, hot summer's day. Among other attractions, we had visited the Potsdam palaces and in the evening had a refreshing swim at the Wannsee lake beach. But this August, the temperature in Berlin's streets stayed at Mediterranean levels far into the night. There was so much by way of impressions and thoughts to sort through, questions to ask, and reflections to follow – for instance, regarding the ambivalent friendship between Frederick the Great and Voltaire – and what about that historic-looking empty department store building across the street? When was the last time anything was sold there and what sort of goods would they have been?« (the father's notes) (Fig. 5.5).

112 | Creating Learning Spaces

Figures 5.6 and 5.7

Peter turns the post windmill in Kreuzberg

Figure 5.8

»The DC-3 Raisin Bomber on the roof of Berlin's Museum of Technology in and of itself is an attraction for a nine-year old. The background story of the ›Luftbrücke‹ (Berlin Airlift) set up by the Americans just adds that much more, and we reconstructed it step by step in the place where it happened and then in the evening in the Brüder Street apartment« (the father's notes).

Figures 5.9 and 5.10

»The Berlin lady docent who was on duty in this section of the Technology Museum deserves special mention for the technical dialog that she held with my nine-year old son and me on the development and technical state of early TV sets, even the functioning of the Brownian tube. She combined all that is helpful for a good technical instruction: knowledge, humor, mental agility, enjoyment in communicating and, even more, life wisdom« (Fig. 5.9)…

»We spent several hours just in the locomotive shops of the Berlin Museum of Technology, so that one day was not enough to do this museum justice. We returned for a second day to continue our viewing and examinations. The giant old steam locomotives were particularly fascinating and invited intensive exploration« (Fig. 5.10) (the father's notes).

114 | Creating Learning Spaces

 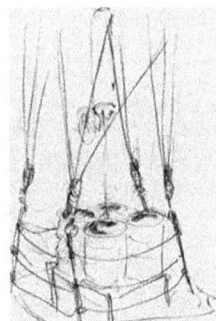

Figures 5.11. and 5.12

»The Berlin Wall Museum has illustrative exhibits documenting escape attempts by people from the walled-in GDR that was secured by electric fences and death strips. Underground tunnels were a frequent if risky escape method. Late in the evening on returning to our apartment on Brüder Street, my son and I discussed what we had seen and learned, and I made a few pencil sketches. Another successful flight concept, this one above ground, was the frenzied crashing of a car through a guarded border crossing point. To this end, they would fill the body and doors of an old car with concrete and cover the windows from the inside with thick steel plates that could stop rifle bullets. A set of small holes drilled into the metal behind the windshield let them steer the car even with this armoring in place (Fig. 5.11). A spectacular escape method, albeit one that only succeeded on the second attempt, was carried out by two families taking to the air in a homemade hot air balloon they had sown together during many nights (Fig. 5.12). While today in the eastern German states there is much talk about the lost social cohesion they enjoyed during the GDR days, apparently personal freedom was so important for some people that they were willing to take the risks inherent in such escape attempts. My son and I tried to reconstruct it all down to the smallest detail and debated for a long time about the complex and basic theme of freedom, including the many politically imposed compulsions that reach into individual lives, even in what is an open and democratic society like ours is today« (the father's notes, chapter 5).

6 Experiential Learning Across the Fields

The Irish philosopher John O'Donohue writes in his book »Anam Cara« (1997, p. 207): »Autumn is one of my favourite times of the year; seeds sown in the spring, nurtured by the summer, now yield their fruit in autumn. It is harvest, the homecoming of the seeds' long and lonely journey through darkness and silence under the earth's surface... Correspondingly, when it is autumn in your life, the things that happened in the past, or the experiences that were sown in the clay of your heart, almost unknown to you, now yield their fruit. Autumntime in a person's life can be a time of great gathering. It is a time for harvesting the fruits of your experiences.«

Anyone who accumulated wide ranging experiences in teaching faces a creative choice in putting that legacy to paper. The author in this case chose to use a series of photos with text to illustrate formative and inspirational moments from his several decades as a dedicated teacher, and father. His account begins with university studies in special education and gifted education, followed by years of teaching school while living a rich family life with his wife and two boys, and it ends with his pedagogical research activities in the field of higher education coupled, in part, with retrospective reflections during these later years. The chapter closes with selected material from an intergenerational learning project that served to put the author in touch once more with his own roots.

116 | Creating Learning Spaces

Figures 6.1-6.3

A touch of Italian ease wafts through this Cologne rear courtyard. These were the student years, a time of transition, of loosening old familial ties, of experimenting and taking soundings, of exploring and testing ways, that ranged from art through meditation to psychoanalysis, and of dealing with emerging life themes. Throughout, it was also a time for earning educational qualifications, markers on the way to building both his professional and personal lives (Fig. 6.1). We traveled light as we explored Italy's Renaissance towns and art treasures, from Tuscany to Sicily. Financial resources may have been very tight, but it was also a time of great freedom and youthful joy. Studying pedagogy at the university of the 1980s was a wide open expanse, with great substantive possibilities, from the writings of Erich Fromm (»To Have or to Be?« or »The Art of Loving«) to those of Henry Miller (e.g., »Plexus«), or Vladimir Nabokov (e.g., »Ada or Ardor«), all books that we carried in our rucksacks (Fig. 6.2 and 6.3).

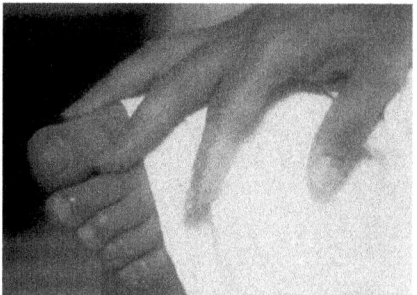

Figures 6.4 and 6.5

The Balearic Islands and Italian coasts at times also became places for contemplative inquiry by artistic means. Back then, I experienced time as a *here and now* that could run on practically forever. The professional life of a special education teacher that I would embrace after matriculating at the University of Cologne still lay far in the future and had hardly any definite contours. With the student life in Cologne also having its share of hardships while working as a waiter and night shift taxi driver to earn a living, those sojourns by the Mediterranean served to plumb and capture the pauses in my biography. They let me merge with time (Fig. 6.4). The 1980s were the time of the therapeutic society. Self-discovery in realms like yoga, meditation, Zen, Tai Chi and breathing or bioenergetics therapies all belonged to the trove of experiences of many university students in those days. Starting from Carl Rogers' pedagogy of freedom, it was thus not much of a leap to even more liberated designs (e.g., the philosophies of Swami Muktananda, S.N. Goenka, or Bhagwan Shree Rajneesh, later: Osho) – and to why these ideas, experiences and concepts should not also benefit children and youths with emotional, social and behavioral difficulties? Contemporaneously, within humanistic psychology there developed the so-called holistic or gestalt therapeutic action models (e.g., Fritz Perls) extending to music therapeutic or body-centered spiritual approaches. These currents also found their expression in German pedagogies. A friend (Prerna) sent me the picture (Fig. 6.5) with greetings from her workshop in Bhagwan´s ashram in Puna, India, where she did studies in meditation and creative arts.

118 | Creating Learning Spaces

Figures 6.6 and 6.7

Scenes from inclusive German-French-Polish-Hungarian summer camps for youngsters and young adults with and without disabilities that we conducted near Passau in Lower Bavaria. Visually-, physically-, and mentally-challenged young people augmented each other with their respective abilities, learned also to communicate across language barriers and to work toward shared goals. The Grimm Brothers fairy tale of the Bremen town musicians provided inspiration for the hands-on oriented project activities. Bettina von Grandidier and I, joined by a small team of other university students, led these inclusive summer camps for the erew-Academy Viersen, Germany (with Eva Kluge and Karl-Josef Kluge as directors), with support from the Franco-German Youth Office, and in cooperation with the University of Cologne (Department for Special Education). Richard, a colleague from a special education institution in French Alsace, seen here in Fig. 6.7, was a dependable collaboration partner during three summers in the practical implementation of the camp and in completing projects. He was always ready to pitch in with energy, perseverance, ideas and humor.

Figures 6.8.-6.10

Considering that I am the son and grandson of South Westphalian blacksmiths, as were many generations before – including the two great-uncles who emigrated to the United States around 1850 – it was in some ways a poignant social and cultural leap when, in 1984, I flew to Michigan to work in David P. Weikart's HighScope International Summer Camp. Here I took on teaching duties and the occasional art project with highly motivated young people from around the world. Young people from all over the United States, from South America, Asia, and Europe lived and worked in the HighScope Camp with a team of dedicated counselors. The workshop that David P. Weikart founded in the 1960s, together with his wife Phyllis, was all about thinking productively, designing creatively, and building constructively while developing shared ideas and social responsibility (Broecher 2015 a). After the two months in Michigan I explored parts of the United States.

120 | Creating Learning Spaces

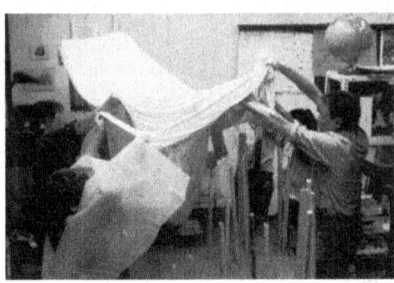
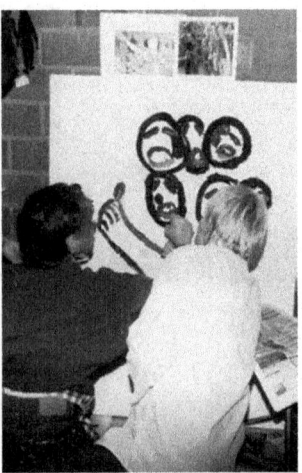

Figures 6.11 and 6.12

Here from my student teaching days in Solingen, Germany, is a picture of students in a classroom for youth with emotional and behavioral difficulties I engaged with in hands-on learning. Using wood, sheets, and plaster of Paris, together we built a model of a specific Alpine region, the area around the Zugspitze Mountain. We calculated the altitude relationships, the height of the mountain tops, the distances between the individual mountains and then transferred them to our home-made model. Finally, we added detailed features such as mountain lakes, trees, shrubs, huts, summit stations and ropeways (Fig. 6.11).

Inviting artists to take part in pedagogical work at school can open up new perspectives. This student with behavioral and learning difficulties is working with artist Gunhild Lorenzen on the subject of right-wing violence. The youth had fled with his family to Germany from the Balkan wars. Anti-foreigner tendencies in German society in the mid-1990s gave rise to fears in the boy that he is expressing here and reflecting on together with the artist (Fig. 6.12).

Experiential Learning Across the Fields | 121

Figures 6.13 and 6.14

The snapshot on the left came to be when I developed a thematic framework for a hands-on learning project in a specialized classroom for students with emotional and behavioral difficulties that I based on the Grimm Brothers' children's and household tales. We knocked together a witch's house using discarded construction wood and knocked-down old furniture that we then could crawl into and read fairy tales out loud. Building the shack offered a rich array of chances to communicate but also of technical-practical learning. Since only one student in that learning group had an intact father relationship, for the rest of the boys I facilitated some belated experiences that they otherwise might have experienced in a family environment with an active father of their own (Fig. 6.13).

In Mark Twain's »Tom Sawyer«, the hero lets the other village kids give him their little treasures in return for *allowing* them to help him paint a long wooden fence. It was a very unusual deal that astonishes today's children. Still, this literary work provides a motivational instruction to pay attention to the little treasures that children, learning in an inclusive setting in elementary school, keep in their junk drawer. A little museum can easily be arranged with them, in a paper-lined shoe box top. A story goes with every object that a child contributes that can be shared, verbally and in writing (Fig. 6.14).

122 | Creating Learning Spaces

Figure 6.15 and 6.16

What grammar school boy would not enthuse over King Arthur and the Holy Grail, over knights jousting and what it was like to live in a castle? The same holds true in a specialized school for boys with emotional and behavioral difficulties shown here. We lined two walls of our classroom with butcher paper which we then covered with Middle Age-type imagery. In play scenes, the boys used halberds, shields, capes and other props, some of which they had made. I started the instructional units with a general overview of works of art or movies that might show a market in the Middle Ages, for example, or by playing recordings of typical music of the times. A collection of picture- and non-fiction books, such as an account of the training a squire or knight had to undergo or of life in a castle, let the boys access the topic individually and in depth (Fig. 6.15).

The photo on the right shows a class scene from an alternative school for students with emotional, behavioral and learning problems. The immediate object was a reenactment of the »Snow White« fairy tale. The students could make use of a stock of clothing, shoes, bags and other props. In this scene, the play acting had suddenly achieved its own dynamic of enacting the birth of a child. The back story for this was that a student had experienced just such an event in his family. In this way, the subjective contents of the students' real lives find their expression in an instructional setting that offers the means and room for play (Fig. 6.16).

Experiential Learning Across the Fields | 123

Figure 6.17

A good way to start a conversation with youngsters (and also with university students in pre-service teacher education), whose educational biography and way through life are marred by the multiple burdens, conflicts, and crises that we frequently encounter in the context of emotional and behavioral difficulties, is by joining them in reconstructing their cultural orientations (e.g., from the world of Hip Hop and Rap) in the form of pictorial design or text or music productions. What takes place behind the surface of their behavior in terms of identity-forming and emotional processes becomes visible, at least incrementally, and, within limits, accessible to pedagogical thinking and adaptation (Broecher et al., 2017).

124 | Creating Learning Spaces

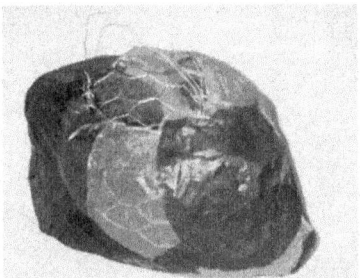

Figures 6.18 and 6.19

I made the hand puppet on the left from a wooden spoon, a bit of fabric and a piece of rabbit fur. I used it over the years in the field of special education and inclusive education, particularly when working with young children. With this little fellow, I would get children talking who at first did not communicate with anyone. Children who seemed to tune out or ignore their teacher's verbal messages paid attention to what the puppet poised on my hand had to say, and eventually they also responded to it (Fig. 6.18).

That a boy in third grade who at times exhibits severe behavioral problems is nevertheless capable of special creative achievements – as long as he is intensively supervised and constructively counseled and supported in his strengths and abilities – is shown by this highly original purse lantern that he designed. He fashioned it from chicken wire on which he then pasted translucent colored paper. He proudly carried his lantern in the St. Martin's Day parade that the school put on in the city neighborhood (Fig. 6.19).

Experiential Learning Across the Fields | 125

Figures 6.20 and 6.21

Children want to test themselves and master real, meaningful tasks. In doing so, they come to know and train their strengths. The expansion and remodeling of our house and yard (in the »Bergisches Land«, a rural region east of Cologne, Germany) here proceeds as a multigenerational project that even grandfather helps out with and serves in as role model for his grandchildren. In later life, after the boys complete their studies, they may very well play a role as engineers in the construction of buildings, bridges or train trestles. Here, together with father and grandfather, the action involves pouring concrete for several superposed stair steps. It may even be possible to talk of precocious project experience, practice in teamwork and acquisition of materials as well as technical-artisanal capabilities as being part of it.

126 | Creating Learning Spaces

Figures 6.22-6.23

Contemporaneous with my work during the 1990s in specialized schools for children and youth with emotional and behavioral difficulties, I taught a recurring continuing education course focused on the creative arts. It was an in-service training program for individuals who had already been active in social and pedagogical fields for some time. This activity as group moderator over the years put me in touch with many fascinating people versed in life and their professions. All along, it was I who also learned in these workshops.

Together, the participants in these creative arts workshops and I worked through an abundance of living-learning processes. As action guide framework models served the »Encounter Groups« that Carl Rogers had led at one time as did Ruth Cohn's »Theme-focused Interaction«. I always emerged from these seminars newly inspired and energized to return to my own classrooms in specialized schools for youth with emotional and behavioral difficulties.

Figure 6.24

Be it Campania, the Basilicata, Apulia, Calabria, Sardinia or Sicily, southern Italy was and remained throughout the years of teaching school a longed-for destination, a world to retreat to, to slow down in, to contemplate it all from – a counter world to my solid-booked professional and familial existence. One time I traveled to Procida, Ischia or Capri, always combining it with a shorter stay in Naples; another time it was to Bari, Monopoli, or Lecce. Learning the Italian language also served this tapping into and navigating this alternate world. The murals I discovered on one of these journeys in the small coastal town of Diamante, Calabria, reflected at once the story of economic and social hardships of my cherished »Mezzogiorno« and the resulting great wave of emigration to the United States that took off in the 19th century.

128 | Creating Learning Spaces

Figures 6.25 and 6.26

It was a hugely engrossing project, building a little hut of sticks, branches, and twigs with our children and the children of our village neighbors. The children readily picked up on my suggestions regarding construction technique, as in how to weave the differing materials together. At the same time, they also tried to figure out on their own how to fasten sticks together. The children's motivation to pitch in was naturally present; there was no need for psychological tricks to bring it out or give it wings. The motivation was simply there and plenty of it. Overgrown by now with bean tendrils, the little shack the children and I built with sticks and branches has become their space for play and fantasy.

Experiential Learning Across the Fields | 129

Figures 6.27 and 6.28

In many spots on the beaches of the Île d'Oléron the children found stones worn round and flat that they stacked up in fantastic stone towers. Stacking and building high seems to be a concept that is naturally present in the child and emerges unprompted. Stacking stones on the one hand has the traits of an absorbing game, but at the same time material properties and physical laws have to be investigated and factored in (Fig. 6.28)

Next to diverse stone towers, my younger son erected a kind of labyrinth of stones. The question remains in the air: is this an archetypal motif in us or is there an external stimulus for it? With the stick end, which easily could be thought of as an arm extension, the youngster taps along between the stones to explore the possible routes, entrances and exits of this labyrinth. This scene, too, appears as a self-absorbed game. At the same time, the action can be interpreted as anticipating situations and tasks that will have to be handled later in life (Fig. 6.27).

130 | Creating Learning Spaces

Figure 6.29

The dunes on the French Atlantic coast, quite steep in places, make it possible, for instance, to toss bocce balls up a dune and let them roll back down to you. While the children initiate the movement, the balls will roll back down each time in an idiosyncratic way, taking routes that partly vary depending on how they arrived at the top. It's a game very much sufficient unto itself, in Friedrich von Schiller's sense, who praised such games as the highest fulfillment for the human being.

Experiential Learning Across the Fields | 131

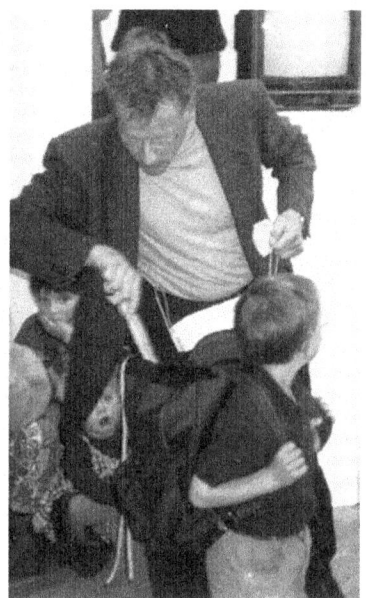

Figures 6.30 and 6.31

This was a project that I carried out with my students from the University of Cologne in the kindergarten that my youngest son also attended. This scene shows construction and sculpting work with Ytong aerated concrete (Fig. 6.30). With the university students helping out, intensive pedagogical work was possible with the children and also allowed them to handle materials and tools that otherwise are often left out because of expense or potential risks. After completing the art projects we arranged a museum exhibition of the created objects. The picture shows me giving the interactive opening remarks as part of which I placed tools and work materials in my younger son's backpack, including a hammer, pliers, paint brush, sticky tape, etc. so that he would be equipped – symbolically – for his life's journey and for creatively handling tasks that he would confront at each stage. A small packet of Band-Aids also went into the backpack, just in case (Fig. 6.31).

132 | Creating Learning Spaces

Figures 6.32 and 6.33

»At the end of a long day on a Scotland trip, eating peanut butter sandwiches while sitting in pajamas by the window, my son is watching the busy back and forth of fishing boats in the harbor of Mallaig and the ferries that connect the mainland with the Isle of Skye« (Fig. 6.32)...

»Even in October, Sardinia's noonday heat prompts taking an extended siesta in the cool of our hotel room. My still youthful travel companion on his own displayed a talent for the contemplative life in how he dove in a very natural way into the long stretch of time that such an afternoon becomes. I then fixed a little snack, made some tea, rinsed out some shirts, and made notes of ideas for projects that I just then was working on, while my older son followed his own thoughts« (Fig. 6.33) (the father's notes).

Experiential Learning Across the Fields | 133

Figure 6.34

On a summer's day under a bright blue sky, with the water's surface a green-turquoise, sunlight bathes this frisky group composed of my younger son, a friend and his children. The bodies dive into air, light and water and build a constantly changing formation that continually relates each to the other. There is something light and euphoric about these water games. Together we enjoyed this leisure-filled life in our region's outdoor pools for several years and during cooler seasons we pursued such happy doings in indoor pools. This water play was a restorative intermezzo in the often tightly scheduled professional, school and family day-by-day.

Since I have an intense relationship to water myself, I did not find it hard to pass on the joy of moving in the watery element to my two sons, supporting and accompanying them every step along the way as they learned to swim to when they earned their lifesaving certificate and started swimming competitively. The public pool during the summer, with its special play of light and color, the coruscating green, blue, and turquoise, surely belongs to the best ways for the children to hit the water, especially when we choose the rather less crowded morning hours to visit the pool. And so often I returned home from swimming with thoughts, ideas and tentative solutions that moved me along in my mental and academic work.

134 | Creating Learning Spaces

Figure 6.35

Modern art, as here in the Centre Pompidou in Paris, can become a catalyst for thinking, problem solving, designing and inventing. Children react completely spontaneously and with a rich flow of ideas to the exhibits, especially when you pick up on their ideas and thoughts right there on the spot and give them additional food for thought.

Fig. 6.36

This picture was taken in a youth hostel in Clichy near Paris where my wife and I and our two boys shared one room with double bunk beds. The mattresses sagged, so that we put some on the floor and used them in this way for together reading out loud and reading ahead in Preußler's book »Krabat« in the evening. The scene amenable possibly to symbolic interpretation, showing as it does, the boys looking out from the still-protecting familial inner sphere into the world outside.

Figures 6.37 and 6.38

Here is a summer garden scene filled with sensory experiences of colors, flour paste and light. Blossom scent and humming insects surround the children. Completely absorbed, the two boys busy themselves in the cooling shade of a sun umbrella. The garden turns into an art studio. By stirring, smearing, rolling and troweling, the children gain experience with colors, paste and the most varied kinds of tools. Flickering light, coruscating color effects – the children are completely engaged in the present moment (Fig. 6.37).

Once I gave each boy a package for Christmas that contained multicolored materials from a home improvement store. There were plastic tubes of various types and sizes, strings and cords, duct tape, metal chains, assorted pliers, funnels, plastic boxes, plastic parts suitable for fitting together like those mounted under a sink; there were also trowels, brushes and much more. I had simply wandered through the DIY store and picked up anything that seemed suitable for creative activity in the garden or on the basement workbench. I'd bought everything in duplicate so that I could tie up the same package of materials for each of the boys. The boys knew what to do with the material, taking this or that for experiments in the most varied connections and situations. At first, some of the materials seemed to be useless until, with time, it turned out they were of use for something after all (Fig. 6.38).

136 | Creating Learning Spaces

Figures 6.39 and 6.40

Amid the shouting of the sutlers, the clatter and clip-clop of horse-drawn wagons, the clacking of looms, the house on Weimar's Frauenplan was not always quiet enough for Johann Wolfgang von Goethe when he wanted to concentrate. By contrast, he found total peace in his country cottage in the Ilm valley. Anyone exposed to other peoples' busyness – how often was this the case for me, even in the small village where we lived – longs to a special degree for such a refuge, needing it for engaging in reflection, cleaning up thoughts, working out ideas and doing creative work (Fig. 6.40).

In Goethe's garden that is part of his refuge here by the Ilm sits this stone sculpture: a ball placed on top of a squared stone. The theme symbolized here is particularly deep and invites self-exploration and reflection. The stone block stands for everything that is firm and stable in life and the ball for everything that is mobile and changeable. Perhaps the merging of the polar forces of *male* and *female* as archetypal life theme could also be extrapolated from this sculpture. True, it took some time before Carl Gustav Jung would take up this topic, but Johann Wolfgang von Goethe already knew, like many others before him, about their central role in human life (Fig. 6.39).

Experiential Learning Across the Fields | 137

Figures 6.41 and 6.42

»My younger son had often expressed the desire to visit Wartburg Castle in Thuringia. It was not just that the castle seemed to him exceedingly picturesque and represented for with all its details an extremely interesting castle construction from medieval times, but it is also known as Martin Luther's hiding place where he translated the Bible. Just investigating this background absorbed in school was worth the trek up to the castle for my son. Even I was transported back to my childhood when I collected pictures of castles and read tales of knighthood« (Fig. 6.41)…

»To wander on mountain paths like here the ›Merano Höhenweg‹ (high path) with a child is not only valuable in a pedagogical sense, but also holds great significance for life. For instance, there are steep climbs, where you have to struggle, alternating with flat or descending segments that make for easy, even speedy, going. Some parts are rocky and when the fog moves in, visibility can be very limited. The boy learns here how important it is to have good equipment along, plan a realistic distance to travel that also challenges and trains his endurance and stamina but in no way overtaxes him and, with all that, he must keep an eye on the weather and gauge how it may change« (Fig. 6.42) (the father's notes).

138 | Creating Learning Spaces

Figures 6.43 and 6.44

Here a boy who until now loved to paint, draw, and design above all starts in a very natural way to take part in the pavement work using natural stone and to test and develop his related skills and dexterity. Thinking about, designing, and constructing takes place with regard to structures, patterns, and forms. The individual pavers have to be gauged carefully for size and shape and then positioned on a bed of sand. On the one hand, there is the overall structure, designed by the grandparents and parents beforehand, but then when it comes to the detailed work it all depends on the child's individual dexterity. Therein could also lay a symbolic deeper meaning relating to one's own life (Fig. 6.43).

Children will very much treasure letting them help in a meaningful, age-appropriate way in real activities. This scene is about laying the driveway to our house (in the »Bergisches Land«, east of Cologne, Germany) with natural stone. The total mass of cobblestones required was substantial, so that we bought an additional load from another village resident to fill remaining empty spots. In loading them up together, riding along on the tractor's trailer, followed by unloading the stones, the boys, helped by two neighborhood friends, were all business (Fig. 6.44).

Experiential Learning Across the Fields | 139

Figures 6.45 and 6.46

The sleeper berths in the night train from Munich to Naples for many years counted among the most attractive overnighting-cum-transportation options during that trip. Here there was much to climb on, snuggle in, and listen to, like the rhythmic clickety-clack of the train wheels. And imagining the train in the middle of the night high up in the mountains heightened the adventure just that much more for them.

Walking the coastal route connecting the Cinque Terre in Italy's Liguria with the children was a wonderful shared experience. Every individual segment is of incomparable scenic beauty, every little scene has its unique allure. Green, blue, or turquoise seas often break in white foam on the rocks far below us. The historic little towns entertain us with ice cream, espresso and other delights (Fig. 6.45). Exploring the city of Venice, with its many canals, bridges, busy and sometimes sleepy out of the way piazzas was another welcome adventure for the children. The visit to the Palace of the Doges and its adjoining prison became a special experience by my having read to the boys the part of Casanova's memoirs where he describes his flight across the infamous »piombi«, the leaden roofs located in the Palace's upper part. It is where he had been imprisoned because of his inopportune publications (Fig. 6.46).

140 | Creating Learning Spaces

Figures 6.47 and 6.48

Age-old myths and symbolism have grown up around the lighthouses that stand on France's Atlantic coast, particularly the tallest among them. Anyone who had Michael Ende's book about Jim Knopf and Lukas, the locomotive driver, read to him or her during childhood can't help being fascinated by a tall lighthouse like »Le Phare«. You climb on a spiral staircase through the turquoise tiled interior all the way to the top at dizzying height, while shimmering sunlight filters through small window niches. Far below sat the corpulent, contented light house keeper with a blue cap on his head. He gave the boys some well-meant advice about holding on to their caps really well on top where it was very windy indeed. Finding themselves at such a height with a 360 degree panorama view, like here on the »Le Phare« lighthouse on the »Côte Sauvage«, and the earth's curvature becomes easier to grasp for the children. The sensation up here is of a near infinite vastness.

Experiential Learning Across the Fields | 141

Figures 6.49-6.51

Living for a few days under the blue summer sky on the Atlantic coast of France serves to create distance from the familial and professional routine, from the multitude of small things necessary to ensure such a family life and to enable it in the first place. Still, the tasks and responsibility involved in the family's protection and safety remain as constants, even if we are all on the road together, as symbolized here by the half erected tent not far from the surf breaking on the beach at »Côte Sauvage« (Fig. 6.49).

To actually be in the very village of Giverny with its old walls and the hollyhocks that bloom here in all colors and shades! It was my wife's heartfelt wish to travel to this wonderful place with me and the children. And there we were, in Claude Monet's country house, the interior painted in pastel tones, with its studio and the surrounding garden with flower beds, water lily ponds and old trees! Collectively, it means an intense, sensory immersion in the world of Impressionism (Fig. 6.50).

Crossing France at summer's end on »Routes Nationales« you roll through captivating landscapes spread out under an infinite sky. Harvested cornfields alternate with undulating sunflower fields interspersed with newly-mown pastures with straw or hay bales on them. Children who watch these landscapes roll by now and then also want to experience them with the senses (Fig. 6.51).

Figures 6.52 and 6.53

Water bubbling from a spring is wonderful refreshment when doing day hikes with the children in the Alps, be it in Austria, South Tyrol or in Switzerland. In this natural setting, the children discover the fundamental significance that water has for us. After a few days of Alpine trekking, the mind, too, becomes as clear as mountain water. So-called civilization with its cultural artifacts and diversions recedes totally into the background. This, too, holds an enormous significance for children who are under way on Alpine mountain hikes (Fig. 6.52).

Wandering along South Tyrol's »Waalwege« was entirely involving. The children closely watched the water flowing next to them, and they thought about the engineering skill that underpins this elaborate Alpine irrigation system. They also enjoyed the freshness that spreads out on a warm summer's day from the cool water flowing alongside the path (Waalwege are paths alongside channels carved into South Tyrol mountainsides that carry mountain water down to the drier inhabited areas) (Fig. 6.53).

Experiential Learning Across the Fields | 143

Figures 6.54 and 6.55

The photo on the left shows my kitchen that doubled as my study in the back of a roughly 300 years old half-timbered house in Stendal, East Germany. Here, in the city of Johann Joachim Winckelmann's birth, also the source of inspiration for Marie Henri Beyle's pseudonym »Stendhal«, I spun many a thought and penned many a sentence. Sitting at this table, I also read a great number of literary works, to unlock other worlds and for a while lose myself in them. From here I had a view of a rear building that had a great hall in it and had stood empty for years. From the year 1900 on, when the house in which I lived was still a parsonage, this hall had served as a church assembly room. Now all was silent – the piano and the organ that stood in it, the cabinets with dishes and hymnal books had been untouched for decades. Of course, you had to climb a bit because the stairwell's rotten woodwork had collapsed. In those cold Stendal winters, fern frost collected on the tall windows. It was a suggestive place that gave wings to the imagination (Fig. 6.54).

I rode my bicycle to the banks of the Elbe from Stendal while I was teaching there. Here I found a still countryside, almost devoid of humans, a singular, meditation-inducing flow of water – just me, my bicycle and my thoughts (Fig. 6.55).

144 | Creating Learning Spaces

Figures 6.56 and 6.57

To explore Yellowstone National Park with a boy and overnight in its lodges brings you in close contact with the primal forces of nature: constantly on the lookout for bears, we experienced the awesome force of water close up and let ourselves be reminded standing before highly active geysers that we live on just a thin crust of earth stretched over fluid, glowing magma. When night falls in Yellowstone Park and there are no media for diversion in our room in the lodge and no air conditioning is needed thanks to the cool night that even lets us crack open the windows, then there is just one thing to do: to listen into the silence of the night and from time to time pick up signals from the animal world and become aware of your own existence on this planet in a new and deeper way (Fig. 6.56).

To prepare for our journey to the USA, my younger son had assigned me Dan Brown's »The Lost Symbol« to read in the original English. While reading it, I was supposed to make notes about the various locations in the novel set in Washington D.C. When we arrived there eventually, we reconstructed the action and beyond that there was of course quite a bit more architecture, art and technology to discover in this city before we journeyed on to the western United States (Fig. 6.57).

Experiential Learning Across the Fields | 145

Figure 6.58 and 6.59

Anyone who delves into Friedrich Nietzsche's life and work knows the significance that Sils-Maria, Switzerland, held for the philosopher as a place of retreat for thinking and for writing. It was not all that different for me, coming to the Upper Engadin with many abysmal experiences from schools and universities that needed sorting out and needed to be quarried for their deeper substance. Suffering damage after being active in pedagogical institutions for periods of time is unavoidable unless now and then a time-out is taken. Its survival value resides in contemplative phases, breathing fresh air, movement, mountain ascents, or looking into the distance. Sils-Maria is an auspicious starting point for this. It is about stepping back from the many small impositions of the pedagogic workaday; about distancing the self from the many small administrative acts which we must contribute simply in order to secure our livelihood. The mountains surrounding Lake Sils in the Engadin are highly conducive places for me in this respect, because of the region's special character that so many intellectuals experienced before me. I visualized the library (Fig. 6.58) in the Hotel »Waldhaus« (Fig. 6.59) as a place for conversation and reflection, for thinking through discrete episodes from schools and universities. The idea was once more to have the various stages of professional and familial life pass in review with an attentive conversation partner. The sojourn in Sils-Maria in a certain sense turned into my »Zauberberg« (Magic Mountain, a novel written by Thomas Mann), seeing that I had sustained during the past decades a series of physical and psychic wounds that required taking this cure.

146 | Creating Learning Spaces

Figures 6.60 and 6.61

Being permanently bound up in the institutional processes and compulsions of schools and universities invariably produced in me the need to leave it all behind, at least for a limited time, to come up for air, to clear the head, to open the perceptions and consciousness again for things other than the professional details and to strip away the institutional conditioning and psychic deformation that can result. For this, a backpacking trip on the »South West Coast Path« through Cornwall and Devon was the highly conducive means. The photo on the left shows the view from a bedroom in a cottage near Porthleven. The Atlantic Ocean breakers roll in right behind those hills (Fig. 6.60).

Human science departments in German universities can at times be very politico-ideologically stamped, intellectually narrow constructs with only a modicum of academic freedom left in them to think and act. Instead, micropolitical tactical maneuvering, power struggles and intrigues often condition the daily academic routine and the work atmosphere. Having involuntarily found myself in such a situation for a number of years, I began to seek out collaboration partners in the USA as a positive counterweight. The transatlantic work, the appreciation for freedom and pragmatism of my American partners reinvigorated me, gave me new meaning and perspectives (Broecher et al., 2014). The terminal for flights to America at Frankfurt am Main airport here assumes symbolic importance, as my own, salutary »Luftbrücke« (This term refers to the »Berlin Airlift« organized by the Western Allied army air forces in 1948-1949 to break the Soviet blockade of Berlin) (Fig. 6.61).

Experiential Learning Across the Fields | 147

Figure 6.62

Leaving the conference hotel across from Chicago's Hancock Tower after lectures and workshops, I put on jogging shoes and ran down the city's wide avenues all the way to the Loop, the city's heart. The run induced a wonderful sort of euphoria as did my entire stays in the city of Chicago, and other big cities in the United States, like New York City, Washington D.C., Boston, or Los Angeles. I reflected that our American lineage, my paternal forebears, emigrating in the 1850s from South Westphalia, helped build this, too. And, of course, so did the Irish who color the Chicago River green on St. Patrick's day every year and make music in the streets: such dynamism! Philosophies, that had the power to help me to overcome and transform the »confining cages« in my working life, which were shaped through the structures in the German school system, and also through the power struggles and intrigues in Germany's university system here in these open and wide urban spaces came to light again. The writings of John O'Donohue, Erich Fromm, Osho, S. N. Goenka, Swami Muktananda, Henry David Thoreau's book »Walden«, as well as the 4500 years old »Book Kohelet«, led me to a new freedom of reflection and action.

148 | Creating Learning Spaces

Figure 6.63

From today's vantage point, it is hard to imagine that this building was actually a village school constructed around 1850. The scene documented by the photo here dates to the 1930s. At far left, we see the village blacksmith, my paternal grandfather, next to him the teacher and his family. In the right foreground is a vegetable garden with cabbages. The smithy was located just a stone's throw from the school. Just what the topic of conversation here was lends itself to speculation. The learning progress the blacksmith's children were making in the school? Or had the teacher commissioned something from the blacksmith?

Figure 6.64

This 1930s scene shows members of my paternal family or their progenitors. It was a community of several generations living together on the farm. This is the workman-farmer ground in which my own hands-on pedagogy has its roots.

Experiential Learning Across the Fields | 149

Figures 6.65 and 6.66

I had a vague notion dating back to childhood and youth that this half-timbered house built in 1650 in South Westphalia was for many years the place my own family on my father's side called home and that many a story had grown up around it. But I only gained deeper insights into these connections when I began a multi-year project (see Broecher, Davis, and Painter 2017; Broecher, Painter, and Davis, 2018) with other members of the family that we called intergenerational and would involve gathering materials like deeds, letters, photos, etc. as well as anecdotes passed down as oral history (Fig. 6.65).

This picturesque threshold is on the side entrance to the barn of the half-timbered house built in 1650 that is my paternal family's residence and ancestral home in South Westphalia (Fig. 6.66). This threshold became for me the strongest symbol during the entire intergenerational research, no doubt also influenced by my having read the works of John O'Donohue (1997, 1998). Someone is born into a protective house; from there he or she stepwise conquers parts of the world but still keeps coming back to its security. Then, at some point he irrevocably crosses a threshold into life, into the world and conquers something new and different, until, many decades later, he thinks back to this once-crossed threshold and to all the supportive relationships and philosophic orientations that he benefited from before stepping over it – but also to the constraints, depending on the generation, that then drove him to develop throughout his entire life, to redesign his existence time and again in the way that Jean-Paul Sartre so aptly described as »transcendence«, in his book »Being and Nothingness«.

150 | Creating Learning Spaces

Fig. 6.67

Inspired through the reading of Walter Benjamin's »Arcades Project« about Paris, and Alfred Kerr's Berlin diaries and letters, also guided by a growing literature about the »Creative City« (e.g., Florida 2005) and about »Cultural Mapping« (e.g., Duxbury et al., 2015), I started to do extended field studies in Berlin, beginning in October 2015. I booked rooms in private flats via Airbnb, in the quarters of Wedding, Mitte, Charlottenburg, Prenzlauer Berg, Neukölln, Schöneberg, Friedrichshain, Kreuzberg etc., to explore the diverse social, cultural, geographical and economic living conditions, scenes, life worlds and life styles of Berlin. Since the fall of the »Wall«, like already during Imperial and Weimar Germany, the city has the image of a creative, dynamic and glittering metropolis, comparable with New York, London or Paris, a city that attracts people from all over the world, by providing them space for the development of identities and the creation of life styles. The driving motivation behind this endeavour is an educational one and hopes to collect ideas for the building of innovative school cultures. Cities increasingly have become focal points for negotiating rights, living space, and access, with many cities balancing the coexistence of privilege with the lack of opportunity (Florida 2017). Innovative projects which explore new forms of ownership and access, collective production and reproduction, right and solidarity, provide valuable impetus for more sustainable forms of community development and public education (e.g., Broecher and Painter, 2019).

References

Abrahamson, C. E. (1998). Storytelling as a pedagogical tool in higher education. Education, 118(3), 440-451.

Agate, J. R., Zabriskie, R. B., Agate, S. T., and Poff, R. (2009). Family leisure satisfaction and satisfaction with family life. Journal of Leisure Research, 41(2), 205-223, https://doi.org/10.1080/00222216.2009.11950166.

Ainscow, M., Booth, T., Dyson, A., Farrell, P., Frankham, J., Gallannaugh, G., Howes, A., and Smith, P. (2006). Improving schools, developing inclusion. London, UK, New York, NY: Routledge.

Algozzine, B., Wang, C., and Violette, A. S. (2011). Reexamining the relationship between academic achievement and social behavior. Journal of Positive Behavior Interventions, 13(1), 3-16, https://doi.org/10.1177/1098300709359084.

Anderson-DeMello, L. F., and Hendrickson, J. M. (2014). EBD teachers' knowledge, perceptions, and implementation of empirically validated competencies. In P. Garner, J. M. Kauffman, and M. Elliott (Eds.), The Sage handbook of emotional and behavioral difficulties (2nd ed., pp. 237-249). Los Angeles, CA: Sage, https://doi.org/10.4135/9781446247525.n17.

Arendt, H. (1998). The human condition (2nd ed.). Chicago, IL: The University of Chicago Press.

Avramidis, E., and Norwich, B. (2002). Teachers' attitudes towards integration/inclusion: European Journal of Special Needs Education, 17(2), 129-147, https://doi.org/10.1080/08856250210129056.

Balke, S. (2003). Die Spielregeln im Klassenzimmer. Das Handbuch zum Trainingsraumprogramm. Bielefeld, Germany: Karoi.

Ball, J. (2010). Father involvement in Canada. Childhood Education, 87(2), 113-118, https://doi.org/10.1080/00094056.2011.10521455.

Balz, H.-J. 2004. Evaluation des Trainingsraumprogramms an Nordrhein-Westfälischen Schulen (Sek. I), http://www. trainingsraum.de/ Schulausw_Trainingsraum_42.pdf (accessed July 30, 2013).

Bassey, M. (1999). Case study research in educational settings. Buckingham, UK: Open University Press.

Batsleer, J. (2011). Voices from an edge. Unsettling the practices of youth voice and participation. Pedagogy, Culture & Society, 19(3), 419-434, https://doi.org/10.1080/14681366.2011.607842.

Benjamin, W. (2002). The »Arcades Project«. Cambridge, MA, London, UK: Belknap Press of Harvard University Press.

Biesta, G., Lawy, R., and Kelly, N. (2009). Understanding young people's citizenship learning in everyday life: The role of contexts, relationships and dispositions. Education, Citizenship and Social Justice, 4(1), 5-24, https://doi.org/10.1177/1746197908099374.

Birdwell, J., Scott, R., and Horley, E. (2013). Active citizenship, education and service learning. Education, Citizenship and Social Justice, 8(2), 185-199, https://doi.org/10.1177/1746197913483683.

Blase, J., and Blase, J. (2004). Handbook of instructional leadership. How successful principals promote teaching and learning (2nd ed.). Thousand Oaks, CA: Corwin.

Blase, J., and Kirby, P. C. (2009). Bringing out the best in teachers: What effective principals do (3rd ed.). Thousand Oaks, CA: Corwin.

Boorn, C., Hopkins Dunn, P., and Page, C. (2010). Growing a nurturing classroom. Emotional and Behavioural Difficulties, 15(4), 311-321, https://doi.org/10.1080/13632752.2010.523223.

Boxall, M. (2010). Nurture groups in schools: Principles and practice (2nd rev. ed.). Los Angeles, CA: Sage.

Broecher, J. (2018). In touch with society. In D. Griffiths, L. Scott, and M. Cassar (Eds.), The leader reader. Narratives of experience (pp. 346-348). Burlington, Ontario, Canada: Word and Deed Publishing.

Broecher, J. (2016). The long struggle to turn around an inhumane, corrupt, paramilitary school specialized for students with behavioral difficulties. In R. Nata (Ed.), Progress in Education, Vol. 38 (pp. 39-72). Hauppauge, NY: Nova Science Publishers, Open Access.

Broecher, J. (2015 a). How David P. Weikart's HighScope Summer Camp for (Gifted) Teenagers became a sustainable model for my later work in special education and inclusive education. Gifted Education International, 31(3), 244-256, https://doi.org/10.1177/0261429414526655.

Broecher, J. (2015 b). Implementing School-Wide Positive Behavioral Interventions and Supports (PBIS) in German schools: The challenge of knowledge politics, education cultures and teacher perspectives. In B. Higgins (Ed.), Goal setting and personal development (pp. 101-151). Hauppauge, NY: Nova Science Publishers, Open Access.

Broecher, J. (2012). Children coping with surgery through drawings: A case study from a parenting class. Art Therapy: Journal of the American Art Therapy Association, 29(1), 38-43, https://doi.org/10.1080/07421656.2012.648133.

Broecher, J. (2000). A didactic approach emphasising the social habitat as an attempt to meet growing social disintegration. Disability & Society, 15(3), 489-506, https://doi.org/10.1080/713661965.

Broecher, J., Davis, J. H., and Painter, J. F. (2017). Rediscovering the political dimension of the personal life story: Results from an intergenerational narrative learning project with older adults in South Westphalia. International Journal of Lifelong Education, 36(4), 471-485, https://doi.org/10.1080/02601370.2017.1285361.

Broecher, J., Davis, J. H., Matthews, K. K., Painter, J. F., and Pasour, K. (2014). How transatlantic workshops and field trips can make German-American university-partnerships an active learning space. Internationalisation of Higher Education, Vol. 2, 18-42, Open Access.

Broecher, J., and Painter, J. F. (2019). Spaces of commoning, in Berlin and other cities, and their potential for the building of sustainable social communities and educational cultures. 49th annual conference of the Urban Affairs Association (UAA): »Claiming Rights to the City: Community, Capital, and the State«, April 24–27, 2019, Los Angeles, CA, UCLA Luskin Conference Center; ResearchGate, May 2, 2019, DOI: 10.13140/RG.2.2.31459.20002/1.

Broecher, J., Painter, J. F., and Davis, J. H. (2018). Life stories from citizens of South Westphalia, Germany, born between 1930 and 1945: Constructed meaning through relational engagement and expression. European Society for Research on the Education of Adults, Life History and Biography Network Conference: »Togetherness and its discontents«, University of Turin, Italy, March 1-4, 2018, ResearchGate, February 3, DOI: 10.13140/RG.2.2.30421.32489.

Broecher, J., Painter, J. F., Davis, J. H., and Williams, A. (2017). Professional growth through guided autobiographical reflection: A case study from pre-service teacher education. In R. Nata (Ed.), Progress in Education, Vol. 43 (pp. 153-196). Hauppauge, NY: Nova Science Publishers, Open Access.

Bründel, H., and Simon, E. (2013). Die Trainingsraum-Methode (3rd rev. ed., 1st ed. 2003, 2nd rev. ed. 2007). Weinheim, Germany: Beltz.

Byrnes, D. A. (2001). Travel schooling: Helping children learn through travel. Childhood Education, 77(6), 345-350, https://doi.org/10.108 0/00094056.2001.10521668.

Cefai, C. (2013). Resilience-enhancing classrooms for children with social, emotional and behavioural difficulties. In T. Cole, H. Daniels, and J. Visser (Eds.), The Routledge international companion to emotional and behavioural difficulties (pp. 184-192). New York, NY, London, UK: Routledge.

Chang, E. (2012). Art Trek: Looking at art with young children. International Journal of Education through Art, 8(2), 151-167, https://doi.org/10.1386/eta.8.2.151_1.

Chang, E. (2006). Interactive experiences and contextual learning in museums. Studies in Art Education, 47(2), 170-186, https://doi.org/10.1080/00393541.2006.11650492.
Claßen, A., and Nießen, K. (2006). Das Trainingsraum-Programm. Mülheim, Germany: Verlag an der Ruhr.
Clarke, M., and Drudy, S. (2006). Teaching for diversity, social justice and global awareness. European Journal of Teacher Education, 29 (3), 371-386, https://doi.org/10.1080/02619760600795239.
Cole, T., Daniels, H., and Visser, J. (2013). The Routledge international companion to emotional and behavioral difficulties. New York, NY: Routledge.
Cole, C.L., and Levinson, T.R. (2002). Effects of with-in-activity choices on the challenging behavior of children with severe developmental disabilities. Journal of Positive Behavior Interventions, 4(1), 29-37, 52, https://doi.org/10.1177/109830070200400106.
Colley, D. (2009). Nurture groups in secondary schools. Emotional and Behavioural Difficulties, 14(4), 291-300, https://doi.org/10.1080/13632750903303120.
Conroy, M. A., Alter, P. J., and Sutherland, K. (2014). Classroom-based intervention research in the field of EBD. In P. Garner, J. M. Kauffman, and M. Elliott (Eds.), The Sage handbook of emotional and behavioral difficulties (2nd ed., pp. 465-477). Los Angeles, CA, London, UK: Sage, https://doi.org/10.4135/9781446247525.n34.
Cooper, P. (2011). Teacher strategies for effective intervention with students presenting social, emotional and behavioural difficulties: An international review. European Journal of Special Needs Education, 26(1), 71-86, https://doi.org/10.1080/08856257.2011.543547.
Croll, P., and Moses, D. (2000). Ideologies and utopias. European Journal of Special Needs Education, 15(1), 1-12, https://doi.org/10.1080/088562500361664.
Csikszentmihalyi, M. (2008). Flow: The psychology of optimal experience. New York, NY: Harper & Row.
Dieker, L. A., and Monda-Amaya, L. E. (1995). Reflective teaching: A process for analyzing journals of preservice educators. Teacher Edu-

cation and Special Education, 18(4), 240-252, https://doi.org/10.117
7/088840649501800404.

Downer, J., Campos, R., McWayne, C., and Gartner, T. (2008). Father involvement and children's early learning. Marriage & Family Review, 43(1), 67-108, https://doi.org/10.1080/01494920802010264.

Doyle, R. (2003). Developing the nurturing school. Emotional and Behavioural Difficulties, 8(4), 252-266, https://doi.org/10.1080/13632 750300507024.

Durko, A.M., and Petrick, J.F. (2013). Family and relationship benefits of travel experiences. Journal of Travel Research, 52(6), 720-730, https://doi.org/10.1177/0047287513496478.

Duxbury, N., Garrett-Petts, W.F., and MacLennan, D. (Eds.) (2015). Cultural mapping as cultural inquiry. New York, NY, London, UK: Routledge.

Eber, L., and Keenan, S. (2004). Collaboration with other agencies. In R.B. Rutherford, M.M. Quinn, and S.R. Mathur (Eds.), Research in emotional and behavioral disorders (pp. 502-516). New York, NY: Guilford.

Eggeben, D., and Knoester, C. (2001). Does fatherhood matter for men? Journal of Marriage and Family, 63(2), 381-393, https://doi.org/10.1 111/j.1741-3737.2001.00381.x.

Eisenhardt, K.M., and Graebner, M.E. (2007). Theory building from cases. Academy of Management Journal, 50, 25-32, https://doi.org/10. 5465/amj.2007.24160888.

Eisner Hirsch, S., Lloyd, J. W., and Kennedy, M. J. (2014). Improving behavior through instructional practices for students with high incidence disabilities. In P. Garner, J. M. Kaufman, and J. Elliott (Eds.), The Sage handbook of emotional and behavioral difficulties (2nd ed., pp. 205-220). Thousand Oaks, CA: Sage.

Florida, R. (2017). The new urban crisis. New York, NY: Basic Books.

Florida, R. (2005). Cities and the creative class. New York, NY, London, UK: Routledge.

Flyvbjerg, B. (2011). Case study. In N. K. Denzin, and Y. S. Lincoln (Eds.), Handbook of qualitative research (4th ed, pp. 301-316). Thousand Oaks, CA: Sage.

Ford, E. (2004). Discipline for home and school. Fundamentals. Scottsdale, AZ: Brandt.

Foucault, M. (1995). Discipline and punish: The birth of the prison (2nd ed.). New York, NY: Vintage.

Foucault, M. (2001). Short Cuts. Berlin, Germany: Zweitausendeins.

Frick, J. E., and Frick, W. C. (2010). An ethic of connectedness. Education, Citizenship and Social Justice, 5(2), 117-130, https://doi.org/10.1177/1746197910370729.

Fromm, E. (2017). To have or to be? New York, NY: Bloomsbury.

Fromm, E. (2011). Pathology of normalcy. New York, NY: Lantern.

Fromm, E. (1956). The art of loving. New York, NY: Harper & Row.

Gallagher, K. M. (2011). In search of a theoretical basis for storytelling in education research. International Journal of Research & Method in Education, 34(1), 49-61, https://doi.org/10.1080/1743727X.2011.552308.

Gamman, R. (2003). Sharing the load, supporting the staff. Collaborative management of difficult behaviour in schools. Emotional and Behavioural Difficulties, 8(3), 217-229, https://doi.org/10.1080/13632750300507020.

Gannon, S. (2009). Rewriting »The Road to Nowhere«: Place pedagogies in Western Sydney. Urban Education, 44(5), 608-624, https://doi.org/10.1177/0042085909339377.

Garcia, S. B., and Guerra, P. L. (2004). Deconstructing deficit thinking: Working with educators to create more equitable learning environments. Education and Urban Society, 36(2), 150-168, https://doi.org/10.1177/0013124503261322.

Gardiner, M. E., and Enomoto, E. K. (2006). Urban school principals and their role as multicultural leaders. Urban Education, 41(6), 560-584, https://doi.org/10.1177/0042085906294504.

Garner, P., Kauffman, J., and Elliott, J. (2014). The Sage handbook of emotional and behavioural difficulties. Los Angeles, CA, London, UK: Sage, https://doi.org/10.4135/9781446247525.

Garza, R. (2009). Latino and white high school students' perceptions of caring behaviors. Urban Education, 44(3), 297-321, https://doi.org/10.1177/0042085908318714.

Gibson, S. (2006). Beyond a »culture of silence«: Inclusive education and the liberation of »voice«. Disability & Society, 21(4), 315-329, https://doi.org/10.1080/09687590600679956.

Gilar, R., Angeles Martinez Ruiz, M., and Castejón Costa, J. J. (2007). Diary-based strategy assessment and its relationship to performance in a group of trainee teachers. Teaching and Teacher Education, 23, 1334-1344, https://doi.org/10.1016/j.tate.2006.07.012.

Goenka, S. N. (2002). Meditation now. Inner peace through inner wisdom. Onalaska, WA: Vipassana Research Publications.

Goeppel, R. (2002). »Arizona«, ein Programm zur Förderung der Eigenverantwortung oder ein Disziplinierungsinstrument? In Institut für Weiterbildung der PH Heidelberg (Ed.), Schrift No. 26, p. 52.

Goodman, R. L., and Burton, D. M. (2010). The inclusion of students with BESD in mainstream schools. Emotional and Behavioural Difficulties, 15(3), 223-237, https://doi.org/10.1080/13632752.2010.497662.

Gottzén, L. (2011). Involved fatherhood? Exploring the educational work of middle-class men. Gender and Education, 23(5), 619-634, https://doi.org/10.1080/09540253.2010.527829.

Grauer, S. (2016). Fearless teaching: Collected stories. New York, NY: Alternative Education Resource Organization.

Grauer, S. (2013). Real teachers: True stories of renegade educators. New York, NY: Select Books.

Green, A., Preston, J., and Janmaat, J.G. (2006). Education, equality and social cohesion. A comparative analysis. New York, NY: Palgrave Macmillan, https://doi.org/10.1057/9780230207455.

Green, K. B., Mays, N. B., and Jolivette, K. (2011). Making choices: A proactive way to improve behaviors for young children with challenging behaviors. Beyond Behavior, 20(1), 25-31.

Griffiths, D., Lowrey, S., and Cassar, M. (Eds.) (2018). The Leader Reader. Burlington, Canada: Word & Deed Publishing.

Gutwill, J. P., and Allen, S. (2012). Deepening students' scientific inquiry skills during a science museum field trip. The Journal of Learning Sciences, 21(1), 130-181, https://doi.org/10.1080/10508406.2011.555938.

Haden, C. (2010). Talking about science in museums. Child Development Perspectives, 4(1), 62-67, https://doi.org/10.1111/j.1750-8606.2009.00119.x.

Hamill, P., and Boyd, B. (2001). Rhetoric or reality? Inter-agency provision for young people with challenging behaviour. Emotional and Behavioural Difficulties, 6(3), 135-149, https://doi.org/10.1080/13632750100507664.

Harrington, M. (2006). Sport and leisure as contexts for fathering in Australian families. Leisure Studies, 25(2), 165-183, https://doi.org/10.1080/02614360500503265.

Haydon, T., MacSuga-Gage, A., Simonsen, B., and Hawkins, R. (2012). Opportunities to respond: A key component of effective instruction. Beyond Behavior, 22(1), 23-31, https://doi.org/10.1177/107429561202200105.

Herz, B. (2012). Punitive trends in Germany: New solutions for deviant behaviour or old wine in new bottles? In J. Visser, H. Daniels, and T. Cole (Eds.), Transforming troubled lives: Strategies and interventions for children with social, emotional and behavioural difficulties (pp. 389-403). Bingley, UK: Emerald, https://doi.org/10.1108/S1479-3636(2012)0000002027.

Hilbrecht, M., Shaw, S. M., Delamere, F. M., and Havitz, M. E. (2008). Experiences, perspectives, and meanings of family vacations for children. Leisure/Loisir, 32(2), 541-571, https://doi.org/10.1080/14927713.2008.9651421.

Hill, D., and Brown, D. (2013). Supporting inclusion of at risk students in secondary school through positive behaviour support. International Journal of Inclusive Education, 17(8), 868-881, https://doi.org/10.1080/13603116.2011.602525.

Hodkinson, A. (2012). »All present and correct?« Exclusionary inclusion within the English educational system. Disability & Society, 27(5), 675-688, https://doi.org/10.1080/09687599.2012.673078.

Howard, S., and Johnson, B. (2004). Resilient teachers: Resisting stress and burnout. Social Psychology of Education, 7(4), 399-420, https://doi.org/10.1007/s11218-004-0975-0.

Jarvis, J. (1992). Using diaries for teacher reflection on in-service courses. ELT Journal, 46, 133-143, https://doi.org/10.1093/elt/46.2.133.

Jauhiainen, A., and Kivirauma, J. (1997). Disabling school? Professionalisation of special education and student welfare. Disability & Society, 12 (4), 623-641, https://doi.org/10.1080/09687599727164.

Jornitz, S. (2004). Der Trainingsraum: Unterrichtsstörung als Bumerang. Pädagogische Korrespondenz, no. 33, 98-117.

Kalis, T. M., Vannest, K. J., and Parker, R. (2007). Praise counts. Preventing School Failure, 51(3), 20-27, https://doi.org/10.3200/PSFL.51.3.20-27.

Kauffman, J. M., and Landrum, T. J. (2011). Characteristics of emotional and behavioral disorders of children and youth (10th ed.). Upper Saddle River, NJ: Pearson.

Kavale, K. A., Mathur, S. R., and Mostert, M. P. (2004). Social skills training and teaching social behavior to students with emotional and behavioral disorders. In R. B. Rutherford, M. M. Quinn, and S. R. Mathur (Eds.), Research in emotional and behavioral disorders (pp. 446-461). New York: Guilford.

Kenworthy, J., and Whittacker, J. (2000). Anything to declare? The struggle for inclusive education and children's rights. Disability & Society, 15(2), 219-231, https://doi.org/10.1080/09687590025649.

Kern, L., Delaney, B., Clarke, S., Dunlap, G., and Childs, K. (2001). Improving the classroom behavior of students with emotional and behavioral disorders using individualized curricular modifications.

Journal of Emotional and Behavioral Disorders, 9(4), 239-247, https://doi.org/10.1177/106342660100900404.

Kern, L., Mantegna, M. E., Vorndran, C. M., Bailin, D., and Hilt, A. (2001). Choice of task sequence to reduce problem behaviors. Journal of Positive Behavior Interventions, 3(1), 3-10, https://doi.org/10.1177/109830070100300102.

Klafki, W. (2007). Neue Studien zur Bildungstheorie und Didaktik (6th ed.). Weinheim, Basel: Beltz.

Klein, R. (2000). West Walker Primary School, Newcastle: And finds a school bringing new hope to a demoralised community. Improving Schools, 3(2), 18-21, https://journals.sagepub.com/doi/10.1177/136548020000300203.

Klemm, K., and Preuss-Lausitz, U. (2011). Auf dem Weg zur schulischen Inklusion in Nordrhein-Westfalen. Empfehlungen zur Umsetzung der UN-Behindertenrechtskonvention im Bereich der allgemeinen Schulen. Ministerium für Schule und Weiterbildung NRW. (accessed July 30, 2013).

Kniveton, B. (2004). Adolescent perceptions of the importance of teachers as a therapeutic support in coping with their problems. Emotional and Behavioural Difficulties, 9(4), 239-248, https://doi.org/10.1177/1363275204050370.

Lane, K. L., Menzies, H. M., Oakes, W. P., Zorigian, K., and Germer, K. A. (2014). Professional development in EBD: What is most effective in supporting teachers? In P. Garner, and J. M. Elliott (Eds.), The Sage handbook of emotional and behavioral difficulties (2nd ed., pp. 415-425). Los Angeles, CA, London, UK, New Delhi, India: Sage, https://doi.org/10.4135/9781446247525.n30.

Lawson, H., Parker, M., and Sikes, P. (2006). Seeking stories: Reflections on a narrative approach to researching understandings of inclusion. European Journal of Special Needs Education, 21(1), 55-68, https://doi.org/10.1080/08856250500491823.

Lee, Y.-Y., Sugai, G., and Horner, R. H. (1999). Using an instructional intervention to reduce problem and off-task behaviors. Journal of

Positive Behavior Interventions, 1(4), 195-204, https://doi.org/10.11 77/109830079900100402.

Lewis, T. J. (2009). Increasing family participation through Schoolwide Positive Behavior Supports. In W. Sailor, G. Dunlap, G. Sugai, and R. Horner (Eds.), Handbook of Positive Behavior Support (pp. 353-373). New York, NY: Springer.

Louv, R. (1993). Fatherlove: What we need, what we seek, what we must create. New York, NY, London, UK: Pocket Books.

Luna, R. E. (2013). The art of scientific storytelling. Lexington, KY: Amado International.

Macartney, B. C. (2012). Teaching through an ethics of belonging, care and obligation as a critical approach to transforming education. International Journal of Inclusive Education, 16(2), 171-183, https://doi.org/10.1080/13603111003686218.

MacFarlane, K., and Marks Woolfson, L. (2013). Teacher attitudes and behavior toward the inclusion of children with social, emotional and behavioral difficulties in mainstream schools. Teaching and Teacher Education, 29, 46-52, https://doi.org/10.1016/j.tate.2012.08.006.

Machado, C., and Vilrokx, J. (2001). Tackling inequality and exclusion. In A. Woodward, and M. Kohli (Eds.), Inclusions and exclusions in European societies (pp. 147-166). New York, NY: Routledge.

Malacrida, C. (2005). Discipline and dehumanization in a total institution. Disability & Society, 20(5), 523-527, https://doi.org/10.1080/0 9687590500156238.

Marchant, M., and Anderson, D. H. (2012). Improving social and academic outcomes for all learners through the use of teacher praise. Beyond Behavior, 21(3), 22-28, https://doi.org/10.1177/107429561 202100305.

Marken, R. S. (2002). Looking at behavior through control theory glasses. Review of General Psychology, 6(3), 260-270, https://doi.org/1 0.1037/1089-2680.6.3.260.

Mastropieri, M., and Scruggs, T. E. (2009). The inclusive classroom: Strategies for effective instruction. Upper Saddle River, NJ: Pearson.

Mayo, M., Gaventa, J., and Rooke, A. (2009). Learning global citizenship? Exploring connections between the local and the global. Education, Citizenship and Social Justice, 4(2), 161-175, https://doi.org/10.1177/1746197909103935.

McMurray, A., and Niens, U. (2012). Building bridging social capital in a divided society. Education, Citizenship and Social Justice, 7(2), 207-221, https://doi.org/10.1177/1746197912440859.

McSherry, J. (2013). The challenge of assessing and monitoring the progress of children with SEBD. In T. Cole, H. Daniels, and J. Visser (Eds.), The Routledge international companion to emotional and behavioural difficulties (pp. 161-169). London, UK, New York, NY: Routledge.

Melucci, A. (2001). Becoming a person: New frontiers for identity and citizenship in a planetary society. In A. Woodward, and M. Kohli (Eds.), Inclusions and exclusions in European societies (pp. 71-85). New York, NY: Routledge.

Merseburger, P. (2005). Mythos Weimar. Zwischen Geist und Macht. München, Germany: dtv.

Michie, G. (2004). See you when we get there. Teaching for change in urban schools. New York, NY: Teachers College Press.

Michie, G. (2009). Holler if you hear me. The education of a teacher and his students (2nd ed.). New York, NY, London, UK: Teachers College Press.

Milkie, M. A., Kendig, S. M., Nomaguchi, K. M., and Denny, K. (2010). Time with children, children's well-being, and work-family balance among employed parents. Journal of Marriage and Family, 72(5), 1329-1343, https://doi.org/10.1111/j.1741-3737.2010.00768.x.

Mizener, B., and Williams, R. (2009). The effects of student choices on academic performance. Journal of Positive Behavior Interventions, 11(2), 110-128, https://doi.org/10.1177/1098300708323372.

Moore, D. W., Anderson, A., and Kumar, K. (2005). Instructional adaptation in the management of escape-maintained behavior in a classroom. Journal of Positive Behavior Interventions, 7(4), 216-223, https://doi.org/10.1177/10983007050070040301.

Moran, A. (2007). Embracing inclusive teacher education. European Journal of Teacher Education, 30(2), 119-134, https://doi.org/10.1080/02619760701275578.

Mousley, J. A., Rice, M., and Tregenza, K. (1993). Integration of students with disabilities into regular schools. Disability, Handicap & Society, 8(1), 59-70, https://doi.org/10.1080/02674649366780041.

Mowat, J. G. (2010). Towards the development of self-regulation in pupils experiencing social and emotional behavioural difficulties (SEBD). Emotional and Behavioural Difficulties, 15(3), 189-206, https://doi.org/10.1080/13632752.2010.497658.

Muktananda, S. (1981). Where are you going? New York: SYDA Foundation.

Naraian, S., Ferguson, D. L., and Thomas, N. (2012). Transforming for inclusive practice. International Journal of Inclusive Education, 16 (7), 721-740, https://doi.org/10.1080/13603116.2010.509817.

Nelson, J., Benner, G., and Bohaty, J. (2014). Addressing the academic problems and challenges of students with emotional and behavioral disorders. In H. M. Walker, and F. M. Gresham (Eds.), Handbook of evidence-based practices for emotional and behavioral disorders (pp. 363-377). New York, NY, London, UK: Guilford.

Nelson, J., Benner, G., Lane, K., and Smith, B. (2004). Academic skills of K-12 students with emotional and behavioral disorders. Exceptional Children, 71(1), 59-74, https://doi.org/10.1177/001440290407100104.

Newman, R. (1996). For parents particularly: Let's take a trip! Childhood Education, 72(5), 296-297, https://doi.org/10.1080/00094056.1996.10521873.

Nickerson, N. P., and Jurowski, C. (2001). The influence of children on vacation travel patterns. Journal of Vacation Marketing, 7(1), 19-30, https://doi.org/10.1177/135676670100700102.

Nicholson, T. (2014). Academic achievement and behavior. In P. Garner, J. M. Kauffman, and J. Elliott (Eds.), The Sage handbook of emotional and behavioral difficulties (2nd ed.) (pp. 177-188). London, UK, Thousand Oaks, CA: Sage, https://doi.org/10.4135/978144 6247525.n13.

Nind, M., Boorman, G., and Clarke, G. (2012). Creating spaces to belong. International Journal of Inclusive Education, 16(7), 643-656, https://doi.org/10.1080/13603116.2010.495790.

Nissimov-Nahum, E. (2008). A model for art therapy in educational settings with children who behave aggressively. The Arts in Psychotherapy, 35, 341-348, https://doi.org/10.1016/j.aip.2008.07.003.

O'Connor, B. A. (2013). Multi-agency working with children with EBD and their families. In T. Cole, H. Daniels, and J. Visser (Eds.), The Routledge international companion to emotional and behavioural difficulties (pp. 313-321). London, UK, New York, NY: Routledge.

O'Connor, M., Hodkinson, A., Burton, D., and Torstensson, G. (2011). Pupil voice. Emotional and Behavioural Difficulties, 16(3), 289-302, https://doi.org/10.1080/13632752.2011.595095.

O'Donohue, J. (1998). Eternal echoes. Exploring our hunger to belong. London, UK, New York, NY: Bantam Books.

O'Donohue, J. (1997). Anam Cara. Spiritual wisdom from the Celtic world. London, UK, New York, NY: Bantam Books.

Ogden, T. (2013). Working with parents and families to lessen the EBD of children and young people. In T. Cole, H. Daniels, and J. Visser (Eds.), The Routledge international companion to emotional and behavioural difficulties (pp. 306-312). London, UK, New York, NY: Routledge.

Osho (2013). The book of children. Supporting the freedom and intelligence of a new generation. New York, NY: Osho Int. Foundation.

Panacek, L. J., and Dunlap, G. (2003). The social lives of children with emotional and behavioral disorders in self-contained classrooms. Exceptional Children, 69(3), 333-348, https://doi.org/10.1177/0014 40290306900305.

Partin, I. C., Robertson, R. E., Maggin, D. M., Oliver, R. M., and Wehby, J. H. (2010). Using teacher praise and opportunities to respond to promote appropriate student behavior. Preventing School Failure, 54 (3), 172-178, https://doi.org/10.1080/10459880903493179.

Pattnaik, J., and Sriram, R. (2010). Father/male involvement in the care and education of children. History, trends, research, policies and programs around the World. Childhood Education, 86(6), 354-359, https://doi.org/10.1080/00094056.2010.10523169.

Patton, M. Q. (2002). Qualitative research and evaluation methods (3rd ed.) Thousand Oaks, CA: Sage.

Pecek, M., and Macura-Milovanovic, S. (2012). Who is responsible for vulnerable pupils? European Journal of Teacher Education, 35(3), 327-346, https://doi.org/10.1080/02619768.2012.686105.

Petit, S., Mougenot, C., and Fleury, P. (2011). Stories on research, research on stories. Journal of Rural Studies, 27(4), 394-402, https://doi.org/10.1016/j.jrurstud.2011.08.002.

Piscitelli, B. (2001). Young children's interactive experiences in museums. Curator, 44(3), 224-229, https://doi.org/10.1111/j.2151-6952.2001.tb01162.x.

Pongratz, L. A. (2010). Einstimmung in die Kontrollgesellschaft. Der Trainingsraum als gouvernementale Strafpraxis. Pädagogische Korrespondenz, no. 41, 63-74.

Popp, P. A., Grant, L. W., and Stronge, J. H. (2011). Effective teachers for at-risk or highly mobile students. Journal of Education for Students Placed at Risk, 16(4), 275-291, https://doi.org/10.1080/10824669.2011.610236.

Powers, W. T. (1998). Making sense of behavior. The meaning of control. New Canaan, CT: Benchmark.

Prescott, M. V., Sekendur, B., Bailey, B., and Hoshino, J. (2008). Art making as a component and facilitator of resiliency with homeless youth. Art Therapy, 25(4), 156-163, https://doi.org/10.1080/07421656.2008.10129549.

Preuss-Lausitz, U. (2011). Gutachten zum Stand und zu den Perspektiven inklusiver sonderpädagogischer Förderung in Sachsen. Landtagsfraktion von Bündnis 90/Die Grünen (accessed July 30, 2013).

Rae, T. (2012). Developing emotional literacy-approaches for staff and students developing an approach in the SEBD school. In J. Visser, H. Daniels, and T. Cole (Eds.), Transforming troubled lives (pp. 1-18). Emerald: UK, https://doi.org/10.1108/S1479-3636(2012)00000 02004.

Razer, M., Friedman, V., and Warshofsky, B. (2013). Schools as agents of social exclusion and inclusion. International Journal of Inclusive Education, 17(11), 1152-1170, https://doi.org/10.1080/13603116.20 12.742145.

Reid, R., Gonzalez, J. E., Nordness, P. D., Trout, A. L., and Epstein, M. H. (2004). A meta-analysis of the academic status of students with emotional/behavioural disturbance. Journal of Special Education, 38 (3), 130-143, https://doi.org/10.1177/00224669040380030101.

Reynolds, R., and Brown, J. (2010). Social justice and school linkages in teacher education programmes. European Journal of Teacher Education, 33(4), 405-419, https://doi.org/10.1080/02619768.2010.52 9124.

Richardson, B. G., and Shupe, M. (2003). The importance of teacher self-awareness in working with students with emotional and behavioral disorders. Teaching Exceptional Children, 36(2), 8-13, https://doi.org/10.1177/004005990303600201.

Robinson, C., and Taylor, C. (2012). Student voice as a contested practice. Improving Schools, 16(1), 32-46, https://doi.org/10.1177/1365 480212469713.

Rogers, B. (2013). Communication with children in the classroom. In T. Cole, H. Daniels, and J. Visser (Eds.), The Routledge international companion to emotional and behavioural difficulties (pp. 237-245). London, UK, New York, NY: Routledge.

Romaniuk, C., and Miltenberger, R. G. (2001). The influence of preference and choice of activity on problem behavior. Journal of Positive Behavior Interventions, 3(3), 152-159, https://doi.org/10.1177/1098 30070100300303.

Sailor, W., Dunlap, G., Sugai, G., and Horner, R. (2009). Handbook of Positive Behavior Support. New York, NY: Springer, https://doi.org/10.1007/978-0-387-09632-2.

Sandmire, D. A., Roberts Gorham, S., Rankin, N. E., and Grimm, D. R. (2012). The influence of art making on anxiety. Art Therapy, 29(2), 68-73, https://doi.org/10.1080/07421656.2012.683748.

Sartre, J.-P. (1992). Being and nothingness. London, UK, New York, NY: Washington Square Press.

Scanlon, L. (2012). »Why didn't they ask me?« Improving Schools, 15(3), 185-197, https://doi.org/10.1177/1365480212461824.

Schön, D. (1983). The reflective practitioner. How professionals think in action. New York, NY: Basic Books.

Scholes, L., and Nagel, M. C. (2012). Engaging the creative arts to meet the needs of twenty-first-century boys. International Journal of Inclusive Education, 16(10), 969-984, https://doi.org/10.1080/13603116.2010.538863.

Scott, J. (2001). If class is dead, why won't it lie down? In A. Woodward and M. Kohli (Eds.), Inclusions and exclusions in European societies (pp. 127-146). New York, NY: Routledge.

Sellman, E. (2009). Lessons learned: Student voice at a school for pupils experiencing social, emotional and behavioural difficulties. Emotional and Behavioural Difficulties, 14(1), 33-48, https://doi.org/10.1080/13632750802655687.

Shaw, S. M., Havitz, M. E., and Delamere, F. M. (2008). »I decided to invest in my kids' memories«: Family vacations, memories, and the social construction of the family. Tourism, Culture & Communication, 8(2), 13-26, https://doi.org/10.3727/109830408783900361.

Shearman, S. (2003). What is the reality of inclusion for children with emotional and behavioural difficulties in the primary classroom? Emotional and Behavioural Difficulties, 8(19), 53-76, https://doi.org/10.1080/13632750300507006.

Sheldon, S. B., and Epstein, J. L. (2002). Improving student behavior and school discipline with family and community involvement. Education and Urban Society, 35(1), 4-26, https://doi.org/10.1177/001 312402237212.

Shogren, K. A., Faggella-Luby, M. N., Jik Bae, S., and Wehmeyer, M. L. (2004). The effect of choice-making as an intervention for problem behavior: Journal of Positive Behavior Interventions, 6(4), 228-237, https://doi.org/10.1177/10983007040060040401.

Silverman, J. C. (2007). Epistemological beliefs and attitudes toward inclusion in pre-service teachers. Teacher Education and Special Education, 30(1), 42-51, https://doi.org/10.1177/088840640703000105.

Simmons, A. (2006). The story factor: Inspiration, influence and persuasion through the art of storytelling. Cambridge, MA: Basic Books.

Simpson, R. L. (2004). Inclusion of students with behavior disorders in general education settings. Behavioral Disorders, 30(1), 19-31, https://doi.org/10.1177/019874290403000104.

Skovolt, T. M., and Trotter-Mathison, M. (2011). The resilient practitioner (2nd ed.). New York, NY, London, UK: Routledge.

Soresi, S., Nota, L., and Wehmeyer, M. L. (2011). Community involvement in promoting inclusion, participation and self-determination. International Journal of Inclusive Education, 15(1), 15-28, https://doi.org/10.1080/13603116.2010.496189.

Sriram, R. (2011). The role of fathers in children's lives: A view from urban India. Childhood Education, 87(3), 185-190, https://doi.org/10.1080/00094056.2011.10521719.

Stake, R. E. (2005). Qualitative case studies. In N. K. Denzin, and Y. S. Lincoln (Eds.), The Sage handbook of qualitative research (3rd ed, pp. 443-465). Thousand Oaks, CA: Sage.

Stichter, J., Conroy, M. A., and Kauffman, J. (2008). Characteristics of students with high incidence disabilities. Columbus, OH: Merrill.

Sutherland, K. S., Alder, N., and Gunter, P. L. (2003). The effect of varying rates of opportunities to respond on the classroom behavior of students with emotional/behavioral disorders. Journal of Emotional

and Behavioral Disorders, 11(4), 239-248, https://doi.org/10.1177/1 0634266030110040501.
Sutherland, K. S., and Wehby, J. H. (2001). Exploring the relationship between increased opportunities to respond to academic requests and the academic and behavioral outcomes of students with EBD. Remedial and Special Education, 22(2), 113-221, https://doi.org/10.1177/ 074193250102200205.
Takala, M., Hausstätter, R. S., Ahl, A., and Head, G. (2012). Inclusion seen by student teachers in special education. European Journal of Teacher Education, 35(3), 305-325, https://doi.org/10.1080/026197 68.2011.654333.
Thomas, G. P., and Anderson, D. (2013). Parents' metacognitive knowledge: Influences on parent-child interactions in a science museum setting. Research in Science Education, 43(3), 1245-1265, https://doi .org/10.1007/s11165-012-9308-z.
Thoreau, H. D. (2016). Walden. London, UK: Penguin Classics.
Tomlinson, S. (2013). Social justice and lower attainers in a global knowledge economy. Social Inclusion, 1(2), 102-113, https://doi.org /10.17645/si.v1i2.114.
Trout, A. L., Nordness, P. D., Pierce, C. D., and Epstein, M. H. (2003). Research on the academic status of children with emotional and behavioral disorders. Journal of Emotional and Behavioral Disorders, 11(4), 198-210, https://doi.org/10.1177/10634266030110040201.
Vanderfaeillie, J., de Fever, F., and Lombaerts, K. (2003). First-year university students of educational sciences on inclusive education. Attitudes and convictions in Flanders. European Journal of Teacher Education, 26(2), 265-277, https://doi.org/10.1080/0261976032000088783.
Visser, J., Daniels, H., and Cole, T. (2012) (Eds.). Transforming troubled lives: Strategies and interventions for children with social, emotional and behavioural difficulties. Bingley, UK: Emerald.
Walker, H. M., and Gresham, F. M. (Eds.) (2014). Handbook of evidence-based practices for emotional and behavioral disorders. Applications in schools. New York, NY, London, UK: Guilford.

Wall, J. E. (2014). Program evaluation model 9-step process. http://www.janetwall.net/attachments/file/9_Step_Evaluation_Model_Paper.pdf (accessed June 6, 2019).

Wallace, S., and Gravells, J. (2010). Telling a compelling story: Managing inclusion in colleges of further education. Management in Education, 24(3), 102-106, https://doi.org/10.1177/0892020608090406.

Wehby, J., Lane, K. L., and Falk, K. (2003). Academic instruction for students with emotional and behavioral disorders. Journal of Emotional and Behavioral Disorders, 11(4), 194-197, https://doi.org/10.1177/10634266030110040101.

West, P. C., and Merriam, L. C. (2009). Outdoor recreation and family cohesiveness: A research approach. Journal of Leisure Research, 41(3), 351-359, https://doi.org/10.1080/00222216.2009.11950178.

Wiessner, C. A., and Pfahl, N. L. (2007). Choosing different lenses: Storytelling to promote knowledge construction and learning. The Journal of Continuing Higher Education, 55(1), 27-37, https://doi.org/10.1080/07377366.2007.10400106.

Wollenweber, K. U. (2013). Evaluation des Trainingsraumprogramms. Dissertation, University of Flensburg, Germany, Open Access.

Woodland, M. H. (2008). »Whatcha doin' after school?« Urban Education, 43(5), 537-560, https://doi.org/10.1177/0042085907311808.

Woodward, A., and Kohli, M. (2001). European societies: Inclusions/exclusions? In A. Woodward and M. Kohli (Eds.), Inclusions and exclusions in European societies (pp. 1-17). New York: Routledge.

Yarbrough, D. B., Shulha, L. M., Hopson, R. K., and Caruthers, F. A. (2011). The program evaluation standards: A guide for evaluators and evaluation users (3rd ed.). Thousands Oaks, CA: Sage.

Yin, R. K. (2009). Case study research design and methods (4th ed.). Thousand Oaks, CA: Sage.

Zabriskie, R. B., and McCormick, B. P. (2003). Parent and child perspectives of family leisure involvement and satisfaction with family life. Journal of Leisure Research, 35(2), 163-189, https://doi.org/10.1080/00222216.2003.11949989.

Social Sciences

Carlo Bordoni
Interregnum
Beyond Liquid Modernity

2016, 136 p., pb.
19,99 € (DE), 978-3-8376-3515-7
E-Book
PDF: 17,99 € (DE), ISBN 978-3-8394-3515-1
EPUB: 17,99 € (DE), SBN 978-3-7328-3515-7

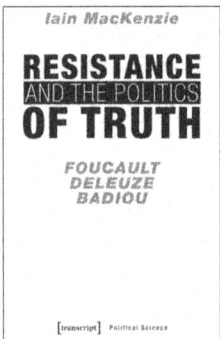

Iain MacKenzie
Resistance and the Politics of Truth
Foucault, Deleuze, Badiou

March 2018, 148 p., pb.
29,99 € (DE), 978-3-8376-3907-0
E-Book
PDF: 26,99 € (DE), ISBN 978-3-8394-3907-4
EPUB: 26,99 € (DE), ISBN 978-3-7328-3907-0

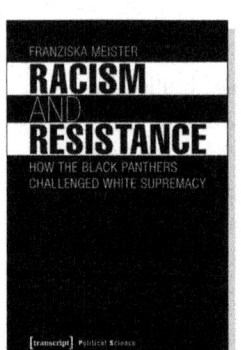

Franziska Meister
Racism and Resistance
How the Black Panthers Challenged White Supremacy

2017, 242 p., pb.
19,99 € (DE), 978-3-8376-3857-8
E-Book: 17,99 € (DE), ISBN 978-3-8394-3857-2

All print, e-book and open access versions of the titles in our list
are available in our online shop www.transcript-verlag.de/en!

Social Sciences

Cameron Harrington, Clifford Shearing
Security in the Anthropocene
Reflections on Safety and Care

2017, 196 p., hardcover
79,99 € (DE), 978-3-8376-3337-5
E-Book: 79,99 € (DE), ISBN 978-3-8394-3337-9

Benjamin Heim Shepard, Mark J. Noonan
Brooklyn Tides
The Fall and Rise of a Global Borough

February 2018, 284 p., pb.
29,99 € (DE), 978-3-8376-3867-7
E-Book: 26,99 € (DE), ISBN 978-3-8394-3867-1

Ilker Ataç, Gerda Heck, Sabine Hess, Zeynep Kasli, Philipp Ratfisch, Cavidan Soykan, Bediz Yilmaz (eds.)
movements. Journal for Critical Migration and Border Regime Studies
Vol. 3, Issue 2/2017: Turkey's Changing Migration Regime and its Global and Regional Dynamics

2017, 230 p., pb.
24,99 € (DE), 978-3-8376-3719-9

All print, e-book and open access versions of the titles in our list are available in our online shop www.transcript-verlag.de/en!